INNOVATIVE THINKING

UNLEASHING THE CREATIVE POWER OF YOUR MIND

BUSINESS CONSULTANTS, INC.

ISBN-10: 1475086539
EAN-13: 9781475086539
Library of Congress Control Number: 2012905802
CreateSpace, North Charleston, SC

CONTENTS

Endorsements   vii

Preface   ix

Part I What Innovation Is All About   1

    Ch 1: Why Innovation Is Essential   3
    Ch 2: Five Requirements for Sustained
           Innovation: Nuts and Bolts   23
    Ch 3: Two Forces Influencing Innovation
           Approaches   37

Part II Methodologies for Innovation   67

    Ch 4: Seven Ways to Generate Ideas   69
    Ch 5: Seven Ways to Narrow Down Ideas   85
    Ch 6: Seven Ways to Refine Ideas   97
    Ch 7: Seven Maps for Implementing Ideas   107
    Ch 8: Case Study 1: Innovation Meetings   121
    Ch 9: Case Study 2: A Method Approach
           Taken at a High School   127

Part III Mindset for Supporting Innovation   131

    Ch 10 Learning Productivity   133
    Ch 11 Self-Esteem   137

Ch 12: Blocks in the Creative Process:
Insecurity   143
Ch 13: Ten Psychological Factors in
Resistance to Innovation   147
Ch 14: Characteristics of Innovative
Team Leaders   153

Part IV Achieving Sustained Innovation   **159**

Ch 15: Requirements for Developing and
Demonstrating Organizational
Creativity   161

Epilogue   **167**

References   **169**

INNOVATIVE THINKING

UNLEASHING THE CREATIVE POWER OF YOUR MIND

ENDORSEMENTS

With the external environment changing more rapidly than ever before, organizations today—whether profit, nonprofit, government, or community service—must focus more than ever before on innovation for long-term survival and success. Unfortunately, there is more talk than action. This lack of sufficient action is due in part to not knowing how to be innovative. Based on over twenty years of experience, explained clearly with many examples, BCon's Innovative Thinking System™ provides the how. As a resource for increasing innovation, this book could not be more timely and practical.

W. Warner Burke, PhD
Edward Lee Thorndike Professor of Psychology and Education
Teachers College, Columbia University

Innovative Thinking synthesizes a number of approaches, resulting in a uniquely Japanese way of fostering innovation that can work in any culture. The authors provide the key concepts of their Innovative Thinking System™. Using numerous examples and Japanese concepts such as *taga* (perceived limits of thinking), this book offers a road map, not only for generating creative ideas but also for implementing those ideas.

Judge James Tamm
Coauthor of *Radical Collaboration: Five Essential Skills to Overcome Defensiveness and Build Successful Relationships*

PREFACE

The demanding times we live in require organizations to maintain a high level of performance through sustained efforts in innovation. Toward that end, every employee in an organization is asked to contrive new and creative ideas that would not be generated through conventional thought processes. Approaches that proved to be successful yesterday may have outlived their usefulness, and what may be needed today is a clean break from the past. This calls for a discovery of new ideas and new patterns in people's ways of thinking.

While it may be true that a layperson's idea sometimes beats that of an expert, the layperson may not be able to convert his or her ideas into something tangible or specific, since he or she usually lacks the expert knowledge to begin with. People also suggest "thinking outside the box" to discover and challenge assumptions, generate alternatives, and change perceptions. Again, the layperson may not be able to go outside the box to mull new ideas if he or she doesn't possess the required skills or basic knowledge. And what about a trained expert or professional? Certainly, an expert knows more than a layperson. The problem is, an expert or professional is likely to find himself or herself stuck "inside the box" of perceived limits.

In Japanese, *taga* are tight metal or wooden hoops that surround and hold together a wooden cask or barrel. This is a metaphor for "staying inside the box" and is often used to refer to people who get stuck in conventional ways of thinking and automatically resist new ideas without realizing there might be other ways of doing things. Trying to formulate new ideas or methods, therefore, requires some new, open-ended approaches.

From this viewpoint, we might say that innovative thoughts are experts' ideas from a layperson's perspective.

Incubating innovative ideas requires some thought-process techniques. We believe that through learning how to arrive at creative insights, how to change the way we see things, and how to choose the tools we use, anyone can generate many good ideas.

Taga are generally at work in all people and all organizations, but few people see or recognize them. For example, we might say, "The demand for this type of product would be poor" or "It would never be viable or even possible in this business sector." Yet many hundreds or thousands of fast-selling products and services are the results of people going "outside the box."

We at Business Consultants, Inc., have developed a training program called Innovative Thinking System™ (ITS) to help people who need to or want to create innovative ideas and translate them into practice. The program has been successful in a number of countries since its introduction in 1995. We have published this book at the encouragement of many participants and licensed practitioners who wished to have our ideas in writing in English.

In this book, we summarize our ideas in an easy-to-read translation from the original publication in Japanese. In publishing this book, we wish to extend our deep appreciation and gratitude to our project members who wrote the original materials and who helped translate it into English; consultants who provide ITS training workshops in Japan; and those participants and licensed practitioners in the world. We hope that, with this writing, many more people the world over will enjoy learning the techniques for acquiring and sharing the skills needed for conceptualizing and implementing innovation.

In this book, you will discover that creativity and innovation are skills that can be learned. This book will also help you to understand how to apply those skills and enable the implementation of your action plan in your workplace. Now enjoy reading about the systematic way of thinking that we believe will guide you to more innovative ideas.

PART I

WHAT INNOVATION IS ALL ABOUT?

CHAPTER 1

WHY INNOVATION IS ESSENTIAL?

In developing and organizing our Innovative Thinking System™ (ITS) program, a number of scholars and consultants greatly influenced us. In this chapter, we'll introduce you to experts who gave us ideas and will explain why innovative approaches are essential in today's business environment.

1. Pressure from changes in the external environment

A prominent US consultant in organizational change, Dr. David A. Nadler, has guided many high-profile corporations, including AT&T, Xerox, and Corning. He insists that organizations need innovation simply because the changing markets and business environments of tomorrow will not allow them to keep doing the same things in the same way.

For example, the technologies related to a single corporate activity are complex and diverse, but an organization engages in a range of activities simultaneously through its many departments or functional units. These departments or units are often interconnected or dependent on one another, and developments in technology in each of them occur continually at a pace that hardly anyone can predict. Nadler says that, without anticipating and preparing for these changes and new developments, an organization will find it hard to survive (1994, 3-14).

This can be said of our own training and management consulting business. Many years ago in Japan, we generally provided training and consultation to people in large groups in meeting rooms or conference halls. Today, however, technological advances in IT, personal computers, and a variety of mobile devices have made remote training and learning commonplace. E-learning is a typical example of this.

News of changes in training and professional development comes to us from many sources, including some of our client organizations. We might hear that they are replacing or switching methodologies or that they are going through budget cuts, with training and development spending being slashed by half or a third. Imagine if we did nothing to adapt to these changes. Our business base would have steadily decreased, and we might have been forced out of business by more progressive competitors. Fortunately, we anticipated change and took early measures to accommodate it. For example, we started a research and development unit to respond to the changing business landscape and to study competitive advantages in our marketplace.

Let's take a brief look at how views on training and professional development have changed in recent times. During the late 1990s, firms began drastically cutting spending on training as they sought to pare their budgets in difficult economic times. The idea was to generate huge savings by eliminating spending on large corporate gatherings—travel and accommodations in particular. The drive to cut spending was particularly strong in the United States. Then the events of September 11, 2001, made ensuring the safety and security of people a top priority. In response, we developed "blended group training." Bearing in mind the above trends and events, we had to analyze their implications and what we needed to do for our business to survive.

While the rapid change in technology affects many organizations to varying degrees, it's only one of many elements of change in the external environment that affect organizations. Changes in the business environment can emerge from any number of directions: changes in competitors and competitive conditions; fluctuations in supply and demand of products and services; trends in globalization and customer expectations; government regulation and deregulation; corporate legislation and changes in corporate structure; the changing composition of the workforce; and, in recent times, measures to protect the global environment. In the context of these changes, every organization needs to anticipate factors that will have a major impact on it, what its worst-case scenario might be, and what and how it can change to avoid these to survive as an innovation organization.

Corporate executives are not always the first in an organization to recognize the winds of change. In fact, more often than not, people working on the frontline of operations are in a best position to grasp trends accurately. When staff start saying things like "our clients are asking about this recently" or "this technology is essential for our work," those at the helm of the organization need to recognize these as signs of an urgent need for innovation. Change in the external environment is a major motivator driving innovative thinking.

2. Important changes in the transition to maturity

In the mid-1980s, we invited Dr. Michael E. Porter, a lecturer at Harvard Business School and the renowned author of *Competitive Strategy*, to speak at a seminar in Japan. At that time, he explained that growth in mature economies could be expected to slow and competition to intensify. He pointed out that this had already occurred in the United States and would most likely occur in Japan in the 1990s. Remember that the Japanese economy in the 1980s was booming, and businesses were doing well, so not many people were willing to concur with his view of Japan's future. In the 1990s, however, the Japanese economy and most industries moved into what Porter described as the mature stage, more or less confirming his view.

Remember also that the mid-1980s was the time when Japanese businesses were taking the US market by storm as American industries mourned the loss of their competitive edge. Automobiles, household appliances, and precision machinery in particular—all strongholds of the Japanese—steadily infiltrated the American market as the market share of Japanese products grew. Only a few years earlier, then Harvard professor Ezra F. Vogel had published *Japan as Number One: Lessons for America,* a work that became a best seller. It's reported that Americans were saying "learn from the Japanese" so often that this phenomenon was featured in many newspaper and magazine articles in Japan.

Porter later became even more popular when he suggested various ways the United States could regain its competitive edge. Coincidentally or not, at some point from 1990 onward, US industries seemed to have regained their foothold to some extent, becoming competitive once more.

Porter also explained notable changes that would take place during the mature stage of industries and markets (1980, 238-40). First, as noted above, he started by saying that growth would slow, and this would intensify competition as manufacturers jostled for their share of a shrinking market. In fact, a few years later, fierce competition in Japan did develop in many sectors, such as the automobile, home electronics, housing, semiconductor, and beverage industries.

Second, he indicated that firms are increasingly selling to experienced, repeat buyers. This means that, at the mature stage, it will be a buyer's market where suppliers of goods and services will have to accommodate demanding customers with ample knowledge and information about products and services. One example of this is a businessperson who has at least two or three personal computers for private or business use. Some people have replaced their computers five, six, or more times already. This means that these customers are knowledgeable and discerning, and they know what they want.

Third, Porter says that "competition often shifts toward greater emphasis on cost and service," and providing twice the service at half the price will become the norm everywhere. At first, it may seem to be an impossible feat, and firms that are incapable of resolving this conundrum have little chance of survival.

Fourth, he warns that, at the mature stage, increasing capacity and personnel without overshooting will be difficult. In the last five to six years, we've witnessed a growing number of manufacturers recording massive losses. In most of these cases, they failed to balance production capacity and personnel. That's because they failed to see from where, to what extent, and in what form competition would emerge and where they would need investment in production capacity and additional personnel.

Overshooting capacity relative to demand is common. The unexpected does happen, and estimates may prove to be wrong. A simple example is a firm that predicts high demand for a certain semiconductor chip. On this assumption, it beefs up its production capacity and significantly increases its workforce. But then demand suddenly drops off, and results fall far short of expectations, resulting in a huge loss. The opposite situation also may occur. A firm may hold off on new investments while competitors start investing heavily and miss the chance to compete in the market. It's common to see a firm hire ten thousand people at one time and then lay off twelve thousand at another time.

Fifth, Porter notes that, at the mature stage, every facet of an economy undergoes change including manufacturing, marketing, distribution, sales, and research methods. When this happens, recognizing the need to promote innovation in every area of operations ahead of competitors is important for a firm's survival. In 1995, when Mr. Hiroshi Okuda became president of Toyota Motor, he said, "Failure to change is a vice." While he was at the helm, he succeeded in revamping the corporate structure during a critical period when Toyota's share of the domestic market had slipped to around 37 to 38 percent from 42 to 43 percent.

Firms that are content with just duplicating the successes of their competitors can't survive in today's environment. Then the question is, how can they institute change to gain the upper hand? The answer lies in how capable they are in developing and exploiting innovative thinking within their organizations.

Porter goes on to describe other phenomena observable in mature economies. Some of the points he makes are (1) new products and applications are harder to come by; (2) international competition increases; (3) industry profits often fall during transitional periods, sometimes temporarily and sometimes permanently; and (4) dealers' margins fall, but their power increases. Again, innovative thinking is required to overcome each of these changes.

3. New standards for competition

Dr. Stephen H. Rhinesmith, a leading global business consultant and former president of the seventy-thousand-member American Society for Training and Development (ASTD), cites seven key strengths a firm must possess to maintain its competitiveness.

First is quality. According to Rhinesmith, high-quality products and services are just the starting point (1996). Simply put, they are your ticket to the playing field. Almost all your competitors already offer quality, but the buyers you are competing for may not know the difference between the competitors' quality and yours.

Second is variety. Customers today will choose you over your competitors if they think you provide a greater variety of products and services. They are becoming increasingly demanding, and their needs and wants are getting more specific and sophisticated, prompting innovative providers of goods and services to come forward with an appealing array of technologies and options.

Third is customization. Customers will choose you when they perceive that you are very attentive to their expectations, requests, and needs. This is even truer today, at this time of business globalization. However, few firms are capable of customizing their products and services for every local market. This means that expertise in customization can be the deciding factor in winning or losing a market.

Fourth is convenience. Customers will choose you if they see that your products are both available and convenient. The key point here is speed in responding. Firms that are incapable of responding rapidly to customer requests are out of the customers' range of vision.

Fifth is timeliness. Customers will look to you when they know your introduction of new products and services to the market is well timed. A fast-selling product today may be obsolete tomorrow. This means that you need to shorten the innovation cycle, even if it means making your own products out-of-date.

Sixth is cost. Customers will choose you if they perceive you as a producer who offers goods and services at low prices. Customer demand for high-quality products at low prices is stronger than ever, and today this is a major challenge for any business. Recently, news of rigorous competitive pricing in the Chinese market where Japanese producers of home electronics and other products find it hard to compete is frequently covered by the mass media. Here again, the ability to offer lower prices is the deciding factor.

Seventh is the provision of seamless services. Customers will choose you if they know you provide consistent and seamless services. Here the winning point is gaining the trust of your customers as a provider whose ambition is not just to sell products but also to serve customers by preempting their needs and desires with new suggestions and options.

In which of the seven key areas described above do you think your firm needs the most improvement? Whatever it may be, it should be clear that, to achieve this, you must adopt new approaches. If lowering prices is your goal, you will have to do more than simply economize or eliminate waste as you have in the past if you are vying for a frontline position in the competition. First Retailing—the owner of Uniqlo, Japan's very successful casual-wear retail firm—is a case in point. This company found a way to produce high-quality fleece jackets at a very low cost, which would have been impossible if they had followed established standard practices in their industry. We see many other firms in Japan that are successful in pursuing high quality and low cost simultaneously. Being able to offer quality, variety, and customization, which inherently come at a considerable cost, requires creativity and innovative, groundbreaking ideas to succeed. In other words, ongoing innovation is essential.

4. Requirements for survival and for the productivity improvement of knowledge workers

Peter F. Drucker says, "The foundation of an innovative strategy is planned and systematic sloughing off of the old, the dying, the obsolete." He also asserts that "innovating organizations spend neither time nor resources on defending yesterday" (1993, 791).

And he adds, "Systematic abandonment of yester-day alone can free the resources, and especially the scarcest resource of them all, capable people, for work on the new." The problem is, many firms are un-able to do this. This is because the people involved in the products, services, markets, and technologies that are to be replaced grow insecure about what might happen to them. Drucker repeatedly stresses that if a business is not capable of going through this process, it will decline eventually.

Now, if you are certain that your firm is ahead of your competitors when it comes to making efforts at im-provement and innovation, your business will likely survive. Drucker's insights and ideas on innovation have had a strong impact on the way many organiza-tions regard innovation today.

If we look closely at the industrial history in Japan, we see that the *zaibatsu* conglomerates of Mitsui, Mitsubishi, and Sumitomo laid the foundation of their business in the mining industry. Political ties culti-vated by the conglomerates aided and abetted the growth of these mining businesses. In the early days, many qualified people sought employment at them. Gradually the manufacturing sectors of various indus-tries developed, and by the 1950s, 65 percent of the labor force was employed by the manufacturing sec-tors. Today less than 25 percent of the workforce is engaged in manufacturing. Instead, the mainstream sectors are science and technology, information, and services. In the course of the transition, the num-ber of blue-collar workers dropped sharply as the white-collar workforce grew dramatically. What we refer to as "knowledge workers" came to comprise the majority of the workforce. On this point, Drucker notes that while "how to do the work" was important in manual labor, "what needs to be done" is important for knowledge workers (2002, 89).

In other words, to survive and grow in a business, you need to know what you should be doing. That will determine your business productivity. Following the same course and the same practices you've always followed will not get you very far. This is a very important point for knowledge workers in particular.

Incidentally, Drucker comments in his book *Managing in the Next Society* (2002, 93-96) that Korea, Taiwan, and China demonstrate much greater entrepreneurial spirit than the United States, Japan, or Germany. Irrespective of the country, the organizations capable of surviving are those that willingly embrace the challenge of innovation. Drucker says that those firms that embraced the challenge of innovation forty years ago or so in Japan were Sony, Honda Motor, Yamaha, Kyocera, and now Panasonic, all of which were very small in size and capacity. Again, in all of these cases, he cited the importance of entrepreneurship.

5. Learning organizations

The Fifth Discipline, a 1990 book that describes learning organizations—by MIT professor and the former chairman of ASTD, Dr. Peter M. Senge—became a best seller. In it, Senge wrote that unless an organization becomes a "learning organization," it will have little chance of surviving.

We believe that there are at least two ways to make an organization a learning organization. One is to conduct on-the-job training in a thorough, systematic fashion. When this happens, the organization establishes a foundation and promotes a culture of learning. On-the-job training (OJT) is training provided through hands-on work experience at the work site for new and less experienced employees by senior and other experienced employees. The objective is to pass on the learning of experienced, knowledgeable employees to those with little or no work-related knowledge or experience. In other words, OJT is a form of instruction and training done by those with more knowledge and experience for those with little knowledge and experience.

So, in your opinion, which firms in Japan are adept at OJT? From our experience, Toyota and Panasonic would be on the top of the list. Most staff at those firms have a strong sense of corporate culture in which people are willing to share their knowledge and experience. We feel that there's a strong commitment to this end. We also know that this sort of corporate culture can't be developed in a short time.

However, we rarely see managers or group leaders at rapidly growing firms over the last ten years committed to OJT practices in areas such as information technology and computer software. Some people at those firms don't seem open to sharing with others. Their knowledge doesn't become part of the body of corporate know-how. Even so, we still get requests from firms that ask us to communicate to these "human resources" how important OJT is. Therefore, we believe that a thorough commitment to OJT should be a prerequisite in a learning organization.

What happens when an organization needs to undertake a project or plan that is new, but no one in the organization has experience in this area? This is where the second way to make an organization a learning organization begins. At this time, those with more experience are not of much help to those with less experience, so people with all levels of experience and expertise have to work together. This usually occurs in development. Then the question is, how do people in an organization go about this? First, they need to establish hypotheses regarding an objective topic a project or plan is to address. This starts with the question "What do you think?"

However, you need skills to consider not one but many hypotheses. And you have to choose one hypothesis out of the many. First, you decide from which perspective you will consider an hypothesis. On the basis of this hypothesis, you establish your objectives and plan how you will go about achieving them. Remember that you may not be very successful at first, since you are attempting something without precedents. If you happen to succeed, be sure to share your success promptly with your group as organizational know-how.

In the majority of cases, failures usually outnumber successes in new undertakings. Try not to blame anyone when a plan doesn't work. It's even more important not to blame the party that initiated the new project. Remember that a learning organization is one that learns from failures. Note also that when you attempt something new, it's never easy to achieve success from the beginning. At such times, it's more important to share with the group what you learned from *not* being successful. Review everything you did, and examine why you didn't succeed. Test your hypothesis to see if it was appropriate to begin with. Summarize all that you learned and what is yet to be learned. Then try the same process again with another hypothesis. That's right. After deciding on a hypothesis, once more set your objectives, and plan how you will go about achieving them.

This is the full cycle of setting objectives based on a hypothesis, making plans, carrying them out, reflecting on the outcomes, and testing the hypothesis. A firm that can go through this cycle quickly and learn more than the competition is called a learning organization. In most cases, high-performance firms are of this caliber.

During the long years of his seminal work in organizational learning, Dr. Chris Argyris, professor emeritus at Harvard Business School, pointed out some of the obstacles an organization faces. The first he calls "skilled incompetence" (1986). He describes this as the state of an organization in which people have highly specialized skills but aren't expected to apply these in certain situations. There's a good anecdote that illustrates this. Many years ago, the Japan National Railways had about five hundred engineers capable of testing and ascertaining track conditions by knocking on the rails with wooden hammers and listening to the sounds they made. Later, railcars were fitted with computers that could do more accurate testing. This meant the engineers' skills were no longer required. Another example is the introduction of inexpensive desk calculators capable of doing complicated math tasks faster than humans, thereby replacing many people's honed skills in math. We are all familiar with such stories.

The second obstacle Argyris describes is "defensive routine" (1986), the practice of adhering to the usual procedures rather than attempting something new or something that involves risk. There's nothing safer or more reassuring to human beings than to stick to practices they're used to. But this mindset keeps an organization from learning.

Another obstacle Argyris cites is self-defense, or what he refers to as a "defensive mindset," in which a person or persons find reasons to blame someone else rather than accept the situation as it is. This happens when people are reluctant to change, even if they are confronted with situations that require change. For example, when a junior staff member reports that a certain customer has been requesting something recently, his superior tells him not to worry about it, because the customer has been asking that for a long time. In other words, the superior fails to take the customer's requests seriously. This self-defense is unconscious avoidance and is an obstacle to developing a learning organization.

The above is a summary of the major mechanisms in a learning organization and obstacles that inhibit its development. In short, if you want your organization to be a learning organization, here's what you must do: (1) remove all barriers to learning, and (2) establish and adhere to a cycle of establishing a hypothesis, setting objectives, applying them, reflecting on the outcomes, and, on that basis, establishing a new hypothesis and going through the entire cycle all over again. For your group to become a learning organization, innovative thinking is essential. This provides the thinking skills necessary for you to pursue the challenge of new, innovative hypotheses and to learn faster than competitors.

6. Managerial trap: success syndrome

Harvard's Michael L. Tushman and Stanford's Charles A. O'Reilly warn of the "managerial trap" (Tushman and O'Reilly 1997, 28-30) that a successful firm may unwittingly get caught in. Before discussing that, however, let's ask ourselves what makes a firm successful in the first place. First, a firm needs to offer something that the market demands and a market environment that will support that demand. Without the demand and a supportive market environment, a firm can't be successful, no matter how talented its personnel, how superior its production facilities, or how much cash it has.

Experts say a firm's success depends on whether the business is compatible with the surrounding market environment that supports demand. If it is, success is more likely. Many firms perform well for many years but do so only for a time. Why is this so? Because of the pitfalls they have a tendency to fall into. As a firm continues to grow over time, it increases in size and in the scope of its operations. When this happens, its own regulations and rules control it. As a result, it becomes prone to the pitfall of inertia. In other words, it's likely to keep on doing the same thing in the same way, over and over again. The prognosis for an organization caught in inertia is generally poor.

A firm's fine performance may continue for some time, as long as the market environment remains the same, but success can quickly change to failure once the environment changes. We have witnessed this on countless occasions. The question is, how can these traps be avoided? The answer is to build into the organization a system or structure that encourages anyone in the organization to challenge any aspect of the organization with a new proposition. This may not be an easy task for many organizations, but we have seen some continue to be very successful, regardless of changes in top executives or in the market environment.

7. Other ideas in the foreground and background

The "four fundamental principles of management value" may be new to you. This concept came from Masakazu Mizutani, the former chairman of the Business Ethics Research Center in Japan (Mizutani 1998, 50-80).

Mizutani notes that many companies focused on maximizing the output of all resource input in their quest for efficiency and on securing a superior position in acquiring customers in the market. He insists, however, that this is not enough today. For firms to survive into the future, there are other expectations: respect for their employees' individuality, recognition of their existence as entities interacting with society and the natural world, becoming an integral part of the local community, and contributing to society as good corporate citizens.

Mizutani emphasizes the importance not only of efficiency and competition but also the individuality of employees and corporate contribution to society. At times, however, these elements are mutually contradictory and cause what Mizutani calls a "tetra-lemma," or having to manage four elements that often seem at odds with one another.

Reflecting society's changing view of corporate organizations, the concept of business compliance has also increased in importance in Japan. In fact, many incidents of misconduct and criminal practices in large corporations have been attracting attention recently. So, how do we cope with contradictions? Are there any hard and fast "correct" answers to this question? Here again, we need approaches that are very different from those we have relied on in the past.

The term "emerging strategy" may sound familiar to you, because it has been a subject of great interest in discussions among many scholars, including Dr. Henry Mintzberg (1987). While much has been said about the importance of an analytical approach or planned strategy, the notion of an emerging strategy as an important consideration in innovation is also attracting attention today. An emerging strategy may be defined as a challenge that surfaces or "emerges" from what is learned through the practical experience of executing a planned strategy. In a rapidly changing market environment, even a short-term plan may not proceed as expected. The market today demands firms that can respond quickly to the surrounding environment, consider approaches from every angle, and create action plans quickly. We know of many firms in Japan today that are doing just that.

As noted earlier, the organization has to respond to the challenge of contradictions in the expectations of management (the tetra-lemma), be attentive to the personnel environment at the worksite, and generate abundant new ideas. The same strategies and approaches to plans and solutions will not carry it into the future. What will enable an organization to forge new trajectories is tackling new challenges with a form of innovative thinking that involves every person in the organization from the top executive down.

Thus far, we have looked at various reasons that explain why we believe innovative thinking is essential in any corporate organization today. In the following chapter, we'll look at "innovation" further.

CHAPTER 2

FIVE REQUIREMENTS FOR SUSTAINED INNOVATION: NUTS AND BOLTS

"Creativity" and "the ability to implement" form the foundation that supports the innovation we propose. Innovation is not achieved through ideas alone. Results happen only when ideas are implemented. Therefore, developing and reinforcing skills in translating ideas into practice are essential for making innovation ongoing and sustainable.

According to Dr. Michael L. Tushman, there are two fundamental types of innovation:

- Product innovation that promotes innovation in products and services
- Process innovation that promotes innovation in the way work is performed, irrespective of the task, whether it is research and development, production, sales, logistics, marketing, or management.

The majority of firms go up and down in their performance. Some show considerable fluctuations. This is fine as long as they stay in the black, but the performance of many swings back and forth like a pendulum from profit to loss. Very few are able to sustain a consistently high level of performance over a long period. Consistently successful firms promote both product and process innovation, and what they have in common is a system embedded in their organizations for supporting that innovation.

Now, let's try to determine what makes high-performing firms different from those that fluctuate significantly in performance. What capabilities or skills do these high-performers possess? In a seminar presentation hosted by us in 1987, Tushman introduced us to his colleagues' thoughts (Roberts and Fusfeld, 1982). They identified five definitive capabilities, described below.

1. Idea generating—Idea-crafting capabilities

High-performing firms tend to generate a lot more ideas for both product and process innovation. In fact, there's a vast difference between the number of ideas they propose and the number proposed by fluctuating performers. This isn't related to the size of a firm. Some large firms generate only a few new ideas, while some small firms come up with a steady stream of novel ideas. Irrespective of the size of an organization, there is little likelihood that firms with a dearth of ideas can go very far in continuous innovation. We have seen many firms that came out with one or two popular products but have never been able to repeat their success.

So those firms with ongoing efforts at innovation pour their energy into generating ideas for both product and process innovation. They also encourage as many employees as possible to learn innovation skills as a routine part of their work. As in the seven tools of QC, the KT (Kepner-Tregoe) Method, or learning how to use a computer, the firms train their employees in the skills of working effectively.

"All engineers are equal in the presence of technology" is a maxim at Honda Motor R&D. This means that good ideas can come from anywhere in the organization, irrespective of rank. It also reflects an attitude of respect for new ideas and all members of the organization as potential contributors of those ideas.

One of our client firms conducts what they call Innovation Meetings once every six months or so. In these idea-generating sessions, they apply our Innovative Thinking Systems™ methodology. They pool ideas on products, services, and work processes from all participants and produce an average of four thousand ideas a year as a result. Meeting leaders then study and sort through the ideas and allocate them to the relevant divisions and departments for further review, such as business development, product development, intellectual property, technology, sales, and planning.

This is another way to establish on skills and a systematic mechanism for generating creative, innovative ideas by your organization as a whole.

2. Entrepreneuring or championing—Idea-adopting capabilities

Generating a plethora of ideas alone will not lead to ongoing innovation. A firm needs the ability to select one or a number of ideas from many to be adopted. Many firms generate an abundance of good ideas, only to abandon them, but some other firms demonstrate an eagerness to try each and every idea. The point is that an untested idea will never see the light of day.

More than ten years, a digital pet toy called Tamagotchi created a sensation in the market; over thirty million units sold in markets worldwide. A junior employee at the firm had proposed the idea, and his manager had adopted it.

The idea for another popular product, the Pocket Board, a portable terminal for reading e-mail that sparked a mobile computer boom in Japan, resulted in sales of more than one hundred thousand units, mainly to young women. The concept for this product came from an employee with only two years of experience at NTT, a large telecommunications corporation in Japan. Again, the idea was supported by her manager, who said, "Let's run with this, and if it turns out to be a flop, the blame will be all mine."

A chewing gum product that helps prevent cavities is another example of a major hit; today it's sold at most dental clinics. This idea came from a researcher in his thirties. When his peers first heard about it, they thought it was ridiculous. Since chewing gum is perceived as a principal cause of cavities, they told him that it would be impossible to sell a product that claimed to do the opposite. But, in this case, too, the young employee had the support of his manager, who found the idea quite novel. The two convinced the company president of the product's potential, and as they say, the rest is history.

The ability to get an idea adopted can be broken down into four basic elements.

1. Entrepreneurship. This is the spirit of taking up an idea and championing its adoption. It's also the supportive attitude of managers who are willing to give an idea a try, even if it comes with some risk. The employee who conceived of the idea of the Pocket Board was initially told by the engineering department that changes would have to be made to her product concept. However, she insisted on her product specifications, claiming that she would take full responsibility. In the case of the cavity-prevention chewing gum, the manager is reported to have said repeatedly, "Put all the blame on me." These are good examples of the entrepreneurial spirit required to drive an idea to the adoption stage. On the other hand, in a firm where employees are not encouraged to propose ideas, and are therefore reluctant to do so, few new ideas are likely to be adopted.

2. A corporate culture that allows for failure. Challenging the untried comes with risk and ends in failure more often than not. Some firms are well aware of this fact, while others aren't.

On occasion, you might find a very capable person doing menial jobs at a certain company. If you ask why, you may be told that the person failed in a new business venture some years before and caused a lot of trouble for the firm. So, in many firms, one failure can mean the ruin of an entire career. In such a culture, it's unlikely that anyone will be willing to take on new challenges.

An example of a corporate culture that encourages employees to pursue new challenges and risks is that at Sony, a firm that understands that leveling blame at employees for failure serves no constructive purpose. Therefore, no one makes a point of another's failure. In fact, when there are periods of silence or no news of note, there seems to be a general assumption among management and employees that there has probably been a failed attempt at an initiative. This may be a bit of an exaggeration, but it roughly describes the prevailing culture at Sony.

Honda has the saying "No trial, no error. No error, no success," which essentially means that people who never experience failure never experience success. New ideas are adopted one after another in a culture that accepts failure as a signpost on the road to success.

3. A mechanism for adopting ideas. In many firms, any good idea can come to an abrupt halt if it's rejected

by a manager. At 3M, preventing this from happening and providing a pathway for the adoption of all ideas requires is a system of giving an idea five chances before it's abandoned.

4. Presentation skills. These are vital in having ideas adopted. No matter how good an idea is, if it isn't presented convincingly, it will not be adopted. *Convincingly* here doesn't refer to technical or other sophisticated skills for making a proposal polished or attractive. It refers to the way the proposer wins support and approval from peers and managers so that the idea can progress to adoption. A project is rarely implemented on the strength of one person. To take an idea to the adoption stage, therefore, it must be presented in a way that will win the approval and support of key people. Without the ability to do this, it won't take even one step toward the application stage.

To make your presentation effective, Dr. Bob Boylan, a leading expert on presentation theory (Boylan 2008), states that you as the presenter must organize and clearly define to whom you are presenting, what you are presenting, and what you want to accomplish through your presentation. Boylan says it's important to narrow the focus of the content by carefully organizing the points you want to get across to your listeners, or what he refers to as your "point of view."

Next, he says that, as a presenter, you should think about a development plan that will deliver the message with impact. While keeping the presentation easy to understand, you should stimulate the interest of the listeners and convince them of what you're proposing. To achieve the above, he advises that you be sure to include the following three items: (1) the benefits to be gained by the other parties in relation to the presentation theme, (2) pertinent data and facts relating to the theme, and (3) a testimonial of your own experience or case examples relevant to the theme. In addition to the above, you must show your commitment to what you are proposing. Your posture, expression, attitude, and delivery make a critical difference in determining whether your idea will move on to the next stage. Your enthusiasm also counts. Boylan adds, "If your eyes say you don't believe what you're saying, why should the listener believe it?"

If you intend to make a very important proposal, we suggest that you seriously review everything Boylan advises. After that, focus on the "story" of your presentation. Write it down, identify the key points you want to stress, and then settle on the closing points you want to make. Boylan is also adamant about the importance of preparation and rehearsing: "We can't say it loudly enough! If you don't rehearse, don't present!" A well-prepared presentation will make your proposal convincing and is sure to enhance its chances of being adopted by five- or tenfold.

Up until now, we have covered the four elements of capability in promoting the adoption of ideas: entrepreneurship, corporate culture that allows for failure, a mechanism for promoting the adoption of ideas, and presentation skills. Unless a firm has people with a high level of competence in these areas, we believe it will be very difficult for it to support ongoing innovation.

3. Project leading—Idea-implementing capabilities

Firms must also have know-how in implementing projects to enhance the success of the ideas they adopt. This know-how includes skills in appointing qualified people for a project, designing systems for executing the project, and competence in making appropriate adjustments or corrections to keep the project on track. What might be needed here to make the project more likely to succeed?

The first requirement is a team of qualified people expressly selected for the project. This refers not to the number of people but to the qualifications and composition of the team. Obviously, the selection of the project leader is particularly important. When conducting training for project leaders at client firms, we often got the impression that there was a misunderstanding about the role of the project leader. Leading a project does not simply mean making decisions on how to divide the work or break down the project areas into parts according to techniques like PERT (Program Evaluation and Review Technique), Gantt Charts, or WBS (Work Breakdown Structure) methods. Visualizing how the activities will proceed is also an important aspect.

That's why a number of other methods should be taken into account. And it's essential for a project leader to have mastered techniques in applying these various methods. However, in a complex organization that also has issues involving political power, a project leader requires outstanding skills and ample experience in coordinating the various stakeholders, motivating project members, and making necessary adjustments to keep the project on track.

Therefore, it comes down to whether the project leader has not only basic organizational knowledge and skills, but also skills and knowledge in interpersonal relationships within the organization. A project can begin moving in the right direction only when the firm's structure is established and organized so that the firm as a whole is ready to give its support. On some occasions, a project may be assigned only to the person who proposed the idea. But this arrangement is unlikely to succeed because, in most cases, that person may not have the skills and experience described above. Yet a project team that includes the person who proposed the idea seems to have a better chance of success, because of the energy, enthusiasm, and efforts that person is likely to contribute. Ideally, a leader of a project should be the one with the original idea, but such cases are rare. This is why we believe the official project team should be organized with the above factors.

4. "Gatekeeping"—Information consolidation and liaison capabilities

The next important aspect is the ability to import and consolidate external information needed for a project.

This is referred to as the "gatekeeping" function. Most projects are bound to encounter difficulties at one time or another. Therefore, this capability is used to assist in overcoming such difficulties when they arise. Acting as the liaison in sourcing information is generally perceived as part of the project leader's role. For example, the leader might ask someone from the company to see if professors at a certain university would share their ideas, since they are engaged in a similar project. Or he or she may ask a team member to approach a venture start-up working on similar technology and propose a joint initiative rather than persist in autonomous development. Or he or she may seek support from another unit of the firm that has recently launched a research project in a similar area.

In other words, a project leader needs to enlist the support of those capable of finding and supplying information that will be instrumental in removing obstacles during the project. If no one is fulfilling this role in senior management, the project's likelihood of success will decline.

5. Sponsoring and mentoring capabilities

The fifth capability is the backup and support that only influential senior executives within the firm can provide. An idea rarely moves forward as planned; in fact, it's common for an idea to be unfruitful for five years or more. When this happens, some at the helm of the firm may begin to express concern. One senior executive may start grumbling that the project has taken a big chunk out of the budget over the past five years but has produced no results, so it's time to give it the chop. Another executive may differ by indicating that the project has the firm support of the executive vice president, convincing the first executive to come on board to agree to the project's continuation. This is one example of how an internal power play unfolds when a project comes under scrutiny. Many worthy projects are shelved due to lack of influential support within a firm, and organizing a project with the support of movers and shakers from within increases the certainty its success.

The movers and shakers can play two roles. The first is to back a project by providing the necessary resources in personnel, materials, and capital. New projects usually overshoot their budgets and are short on staff, equipment, and facilities. In an ideal situation, an influential officer comes to the rescue of the project leader with the reassuring words, "No worries. I'll arrange the additional budget."

The second is to offer moral support. When the going gets tough in a project, the pressure within the firm starts to mount. When this happens, the executive vice president may step in to rescue the project leader, offering needed words of support, such as "If you cop any flak, I'll take care of it." A project with this kind of support is much more likely to be successful.

The influential providers of personnel, material, and capital resources are referred to as "sponsors," and the providers of moral support are "mentors." Both roles are often played by the same person of influence.

During Sony's Walkman project, it was widely known that the sponsor role was played by then President Morita and the mentor role by Senior Executive Vice President Ohsone.

All of the competencies described above are requirements for sustainable innovation that we learned from Tushman's presentation to us. Of these, the first—idea generating—is of the utmost importance. Superior idea generation makes a decisive difference in the effectiveness of the rest of the competencies in a project.

High-performing firms that are extremely adept at initiating both product and process innovation possess the five capabilities discussed earlier. In comparison, we would assume that those with dramatic fluctuations in performance from one year to the next often find themselves lacking in some of these vital capabilities. How would you rate your own firm or organization? In which areas do its strengths and weaknesses lie?

In this chapter, we reviewed the points of five capabilities required for innovative organizations. In the following chapter, we'll look at forces that influence innovation efforts.

CHAPTER 3

TWO FORCES INFLUENCING INNOVATION APPROACHES

According to the concept of "force field analysis" developed by Kurt Lewin, attempts to demonstrate innovative thinking are generally accompanied by two competing forces. One is the "driving" forces and the other the "restraining" forces. Let's first look at how a driving force operates.

Figure-1: Forces Influencing Innovative Thinking

Restraining Forces
-Excessive obsession
-Perceived assumption
-Bias
-Preoccupation
-Holding off

Exercising
Innovative Thinking

Driving Forces
-Not feeling at liberty
-Encountering different cultures
-Encountering change
-Risk taking
-Availability of tools

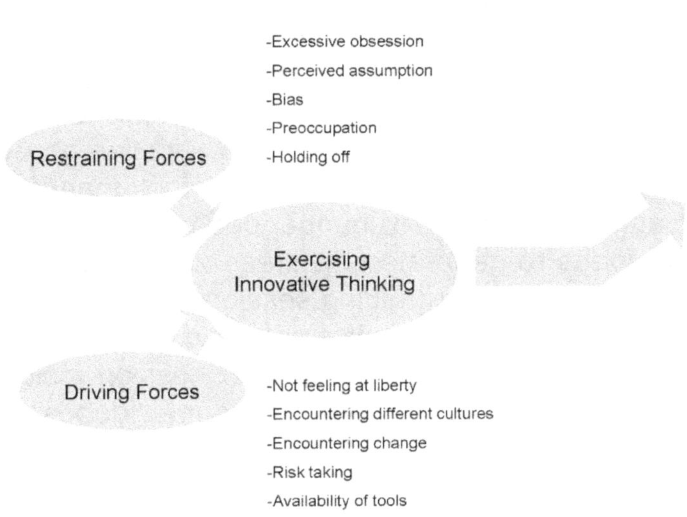

First, when people feel constrained and lack the freedom to do what they want to do, they seek greater latitude and freedom. When this desire is strong, it drives them to use their ingenuity in various ways.

Second, a driving force may also be at work when people encounter a new culture. New experiences often become the raw material that inspires people to create new ideas. In Japan, holding networking events or training that includes participants from various industrial sectors, businesses, or companies—rather than groups in the same company—is becoming popular. The idea is to learn from people in firms that differ in business culture and practices.

Rather than "people networking" in the conventional sense, events of this nature are organized to provide opportunities for sharing real-work experiences and gaining new insights from different perspectives and approaches. More and more we are conducting Innovative Thinking System™ training for the staff of various companies hailing from disparate industries. For example, in one session, participants from development teams of a utility gas supplier, an education material company, and a soft-drink manufacturer came together to exchange ideas with one another in efforts to generate new ideas about products and services. Another training session saw the staff of an automaker, an electronics firm, and department store come together. And yet another session included a combination of staff from a consumer goods maker, a utility company, and a communications equipment manufacturer.

What happens at these training sessions then? The interaction of the participants inevitably leads to exclamations of surprise. Who would think that people from the auto industry could come up with new ideas for soft drinks! What a great concept for mobile phones—and to think that it came from someone in the consumer goods industry! These are only a couple of examples of the effects of people encountering different cultures.

Third, encounters with change may also act as a driving force. Changes in the external environment motivate people to seek and apply new knowledge in response to or as a means of coping with change. We have already covered this subject and won't go into further detail here. However, it's important to remember that change is one of the major triggers driving firms or people to attempt new initiatives.

Fourth, risk taking may also act as a driving force in a firm. Why do you think Japan Tobacco invested billions of dollars to launch new enterprises? The writing was on the wall. As the smoker population dwindles, it's clear that the tobacco business alone will not support the development of a vibrant organization. Due to health concerns, the majority of companies and commercial facilities have significantly reduced smoking areas. Furthermore, as people grow more and more health conscious, smokers who persist with their habit face ostracism. As this example illustrates, people and organizations take matters into their own hands when it becomes apparent that some new action is necessary and urgent.

Fifth, "tool availability" may also act as a driving force. Tools and methods on how to generate new ideas are abundant and readily available everywhere. One of the most popular examples of these is Alex F. Osborn's "brainstorming" and checklist method. Others are William J. J. Gordon's Synectics, the Gordon Model, the NM (Nakayama Masakazu) Method, Fritz Zwicky's Morphological Analysis, and Robert P. Crawford's attribute listing, to name a few among three hundred or more. Acquiring a range of techniques and the skills to apply them can help drive firms and people to innovation—or, more accurately, creativity—in innovation approaches.

Now let's consider some of the restraining forces in innovation. People's preconceived ideas or notions, obsessiveness or loyalties, bias or assumptions can all act as restraining forces in innovation. The dialogue below illustrates how a number of these restraining forces manifest themselves in an organization.

A: (a staff person): How about this as a new business idea?
B: (the firm's chief executive): No, we can't do that. We're number one in the industry. As the leading firm, we can't be getting involved in something like that.
A: What about this?
B: No, that's no good either. We just don't have the right people.
A: But we could give this a try.
B: Forget it. Our customers aren't interested.
A: Then, this is something that might work.

B: No, there are customary practices in the industry to consider.
A: Or, what about this?
B: No, because there are regulations to consider.

As the scenario illustrates, obsessiveness, preconceived notions, beliefs that conventions are set in concrete, and assumptions that something can't be done because of regulations and other deterrents are all restraining forces inhibiting the expression of innovative thinking. No matter how splendid an idea may be, no one will pick it up and run with it if too many restraining forces stack up against it or them. A firm intent on innovation must hold meetings for senior executives and managers regularly—say, at least every six months or so—to create opportunities to review and discuss innovative ideas. At the same time, the firm must check for restraining forces and, if necessary, take measures to eliminate them.

1. Mental locks

At a meeting of the ASTD some time ago, Roger von Oech introduced his concept of "mental locks," or attitudes that lock our thinking into the status quo and prevent us from being more creative. He described ten mental locks in terms of the mindset that causes them:

1. The Right Answer
2. That's Not Logical
3. Follow the Rules
4. Be Practical

5. Play Is Frivolous
6. That's Not My Area
7. Don't Be Foolish
8. Avoid Ambiguity
9. To Err Is Wrong
10. I'm Not Creative
(Oech 1998, 15)

Here we attempt to translate these mental locks into a context in Japan, which is a little different:

1. Are our competitors or other firms doing this?
2. It's a good idea, but let's wait and see how things go.
3. Are there any examples where this has been successful before?
4. Are you sure we can manage that?
5. That's all well and fine, but we have so many other things to take care of before we start thinking of something like that. First things first!
6. I'm okay with that, but I don't think our boss will be.
7. We tried this sort of thing a number of times before, but it never worked.
8. Who is going to take the blame if this fails?
9. We have our ways of doing things. We can't change direction that quickly.
10. We have been doing okay so far. Why do we need to do something like that?

While these comments may be made casually or inadvertently, they can become serious inhibitors of innovation in a firm. From our experience of conducting training for many hundreds of clients in the last five to six years, we found that high-performing organizations that launched many new innovative products showed evidence of only a few mental locks among their staff. In contrast, mental locks seemed to be ubiquitous among low-performing firms with fewer new-product launches.

So far, we've covered factors that might inhibit creativity and innovation in organizations. This might be a good time for you to check to see if any inhibiting comments or expressions are being used in your organization.

2. Taga: "Inside the box" (Perceived limits)

The first step to innovation and change in an organization is to conduct an evaluation of the state of the organization, or a "status diagnostics." The next step is to design the firm's future form or future status, that is, where the firm hopes to be in the future, and then to map out a transition plan for getting there. Or an organization can start the process by designing the future form of the organization as the first step. At any rate, according to the Change Model of former MIT professor Dr. Richard Beckhard, all organization innovation or change follows this three-step process (1997, 60-62). It's interesting to note that, at a seminar presentation to which we invited Beckhard in 1985, he said that he would prefer to start with the desired form of the organization.

There are four basic methods for conducting status diagnostics (Burke 1982, 200-205). The first is to interview employees of various units, positions, and roles in a firm to determine their perception of their work. The second is to conduct a questionnaire survey that investigates employees' perceptions and understandings of the firm's status. The third is to observe how employees go about their work. And the fourth is to analyze various documents and records of the firm.

In addition to questions concerning employee perceptions of the firm's status, some questions during the interview should be like these: What new areas or issues do you think your unit or the organization should explore in the future? What do you think we must do as an organization to adapt to the changing environment? What do we have to do to stay ahead of our competitors? The responses to these questions can also be used as material for further discussion on innovation. In the course of conducting diagnostics for many of our clients, two phenomena became evident to us.

The first was that suggestions and proposals from interviewees in response to questions were very similar. In other words, although the interviewees were responding from various positions and perspectives, their ideas were more or less uniform. As we saw it, the problem was that even the most popular proposals often were never taken up, and people's aspirations for change simply seemed to evaporate. Why? Obstacles or limits in people's thinking. We refer to these as taga. Again, *taga* is the Japanese word for the tight metal or wooden hoops that hold a wooden cask or barrel together. The notion of perceived limitations, often expressed as "thinking in the box" in English, means adhering to or being stuck in old, conventional ways of thinking that inhibit positive thinking and action.

The second phenomenon we came upon while trying to help clients foster innovation in their organizations was the realization that taga were major stumbling blocks to initiating innovation and change.

Because of the significance of this subject area, let's take a moment to discuss the nature and impact of taga in detail. Taga can appear in many forms and sizes, and we divide them into six categories.

Figure-2:TAGAs

Self-limiting parameters preventing the emergence of new ideas and behaviors.

1. "The current environment "

2. "Past events and background"

3. "Resource unavailability"

   -Personnel
   -Budgets
    -Technology
    -Time

4. "Established system and rules"

5. "Blaming on others"

6. "Blaming us"

1. The current environment taga. This taga is often cited very insistently and vehemently by individuals and groups, and even by a firm as a whole, during discussion on how to move forward on promising proposals and ideas drawn from interviews, for example. The proponents of this taga will say, "Considering the current environment, the market conditions, the situation of many of our partners, and the economy as a whole, this proposal is out of the question."

In response to these comments, we would say, "All your competitors face the same environment, and everyone in your firm has already shown support for this idea, haven't they?"

Then, the taga supporters might respond, "Yes, everyone is for the idea, but the market conditions and environment at the moment now are simply against us." This would bring the entire discussion to an abrupt stop .

2. *Past events and background.* This taga appeals to past events or issues that would make a project or idea difficult to act on. In this case, a dialogue might proceed in the following way:

A: Why don't we start actioning this idea?
B: It's just not possible.
A: Why?
B: As you know, our company merged three years ago. Even though the newspapers reported it as a merger of equals, we were effectively absorbed by our partner. And they hold the upper

hand in every project. That means we really can't do much on our own. I think the move three years ago was a big mistake. It's the reason we're powerless to do anything now.

Again, the discussion of any possible initiative would come to an abrupt halt.

3. Resource unavailability. These taga are divided according to resource type. Again, we will use dialogues to illustrate them. First is the human resource or *personnel* taga:

A: Now, let's move on to the specifics of the idea supported by most of us.
B: I just don't think the idea is practical. Although I agree with it and fully support its introduction, I don't think it's the right time. Do you happen to know the number of staff in research and development? There are only one hundred, and they are already way too understaffed and have a hard time keeping up with their current project, never mind taking on anything new.
A: But as many people keep telling us, you know that we risk our future if we don't break into this area soon.
B: You're right, but it's just impossible with our limited human resources at the moment.
A: What about the idea of revamping our proposal and reallocating our personnel?
B: That won't work. The original proposal is still important, so we have to stick with it.

This also is a typical way in which a proposal for a project is brought to a halt.

The second is the *budget* or funding taga:

A: What do you think of this idea?
B: Sorry, but it would need a budget of fifty million dollars. It's out of the question.
A: Can't we apply for funding?
B: No way!
A: But it's still an important project, don't you think?
B: That's not the point. We just can't afford a project that requires such a huge budget.

Third taga is *technology*, which often surfaces in the technology department of a firm:

A: Shall we move on to the specifics?
B: We aren't ready yet. The level of the technology is too high to begin with, and we don't want to run into trouble with patent infringement, even if we decide to give it a try with existing technology. I don't think we're capable of pulling this plan off.
A: But isn't that the reason we're taking on this project?
B: True, but our technology just isn't up to scratch.

Admittedly, the obstacle in this case couldn't be overlooked, but this taga stifled any chance of a constructive discussion that might resolve their problem.

The fourth taga, *resource unavailability*, generally amounts to a "*time* taga." Even though there is almost unanimous agreement that a certain proposal should be adopted, no one seems to have time for it:

> A: I believe you understand that you need to action these proposals if you are to survive as a university. Is that correct?
> B: Yes, you're right. But we don't have the time to spend working on the plan. With all our research and teaching, we just can't find the time.

On occasion, we found people in organizations making claims like these even when they spent only the customary nine-to-five hours at their workplace. The problem with taga is that people are not fully aware of the self-limiting parameters in their thinking. This makes it that much more difficult for them to realize they generally operate in a thinking-in-the-box mode.

4. Established systems and rules. Again, we will use a dialogue to illustrate how this unfolds.

> A: Shall we get down to business with this project?
> B: Not just yet. We first have to make sure we get the rules straight and take into account applicable protocols.
> A: So that means that we can move ahead as long as we don't break any rules or violate any regulations?
> B: That's right, but that's easier said than done.

Firms usually come up against various rules and regulations that they must comply with in the course of change and innovation efforts. Even so, we know of many firms that succeeded in negotiating with regulatory authorities to bend the rules in their favor. Some notable examples of such firms include MK Taxi, a taxi service operator, and Yamato Transport, a courier service. When taga takes control of people, departments, or firms, it's hard to initiate innovation.

5. *Blaming "them."* Again, we will use a dialogue to illustrate this:

> A: Is everybody ready to start working on the proposal?
> B: Unfortunately, no. Before we begin, we have to change the attitude of those people in our group.

It's not uncommon to hear people in a bar complaining about their department and who, after a few drinks, let slip how hopeless they think their boss is and that no good will come of their work unless they get rid of their boss first.

In this case, the taga poses a very serious problem, since people blame others for the predicament they are in and therefore are unlikely to be willing to make efforts at anything new. An even more serious problem is that people aren't even aware of the taga in their minds.

6. *Blaming us.* This is the reverse of the previous taga.

> A: Let's get to work on this proposal, shall we?
> B: I'm sorry, but I don't think we are up to it. To be honest, I think we would be getting in over our heads to attempt something like this.

A: But surely, if we all put our heads together, we can find a way to get through this, don't you think?
B: My answer is still no. Everyone in our group is saying we're underresourced. We have to be realistic. We're just not capable.

It's unfortunate that taga even put a clamp on people's capacity to think about new possibilities.

Quite often, the taga of "them" and "us" get in a tangle. We find this to be the case when we conduct our Innovative Thinking System™ program. It's common for us to receive comments and responses like the following from executives and senior-level managers regarding our program:

I think this a fantastic program. The techniques and methods gave me many ideas for a new business that I never would have thought possible. I now have a new idea for organization management. Yet I do think the training would be more effective if it were directed at our junior or younger employees rather than us. I feel they can learn quicker. Besides, they are the ones that will be working on the new ideas. Their willingness and enthusiasm give concrete form to new ideas.

If we could arrange this training program for junior and younger employees, I am sure we would get an enthusiastic response.

And when we conduct the training for junior and young employees, it's not unusual for us to receive comments and responses like the following:

Yes, this program is one of a kind. We have many product and services ideas in the pipeline now. Still, we think the program would be better offered first to those at a more senior level. They have more authority than we do. Whatever we do, we need their approval every time we want to try a new idea. Without their willingness or enthusiasm, there is a limit to what we can do.

In a corporate culture where perceptions like the above are mainstream, innovation could prove to be a difficult challenge. Our experience indicates that there are many organizations like this.

As described above, taga can be major obstructions to innovation. The psychological impact these taga have on people's attitudes is serious. Taga cause people to decide unwittingly and automatically on what is possible and impossible, and this attitude often precludes them from embracing a positive attitude toward change and new ideas. Thus we firmly believe that taga put powerful clamps on the mind and thinking of people and are the main obstacle to change and innovation efforts in organizations. Because of our experience and learning in this area, we have come to believe that guiding our client firms away from the potential constraints of taga is an important part of our role.

Can you recognize some or any taga at work around you, your work group, or your firm? Once you become aware of their presence and control, you'll be able to counter arguments that begin "We can't do this because..." Once you're able to checkmate unconscious negative responses like this, you'll be able to assist people in your firm to move beyond the bounds of self-limiting perceptions and start thinking outside the box to find pathways to new and different approaches. This kind of progressive dialogue is taking place at many of the client firms that have participated in our Innovative Thinking System™ program. This was also one of our motives in initiating a plan to develop this program.

2-1. Established paradigms

Taga can also be fostered from a tacit agreement to or understanding of customary rules or organizational paradigms within firms. A paradigm is a structure that serves as a pattern or model and embodies a set of assumptions, concepts, values, and practices that collectively constitute a way of viewing reality for an organization that shares these, particularly when it comes to an intellectual discipline or work practice.

When people stay on in a firm, they tend to become unconsciously accustomed to thinking along the lines of the organization paradigm. The paradigm also develops under the influence of the founding principles, the behavior of the founders and significant contributors, and the past successes or failures of a firm. Therefore, the structure that develops also tends to become a taga itself. Understandably, newer recruits or employees are rarely under the sway of the taga of the organization's paradigm.

At the same time, the paradigm itself is not something a firm should steer clear of. It can be the driving force that propels a firm's growth. Hence, it's important that people at an executive level review the established paradigm every now and then to determine what needs to be kept and what needs to be changed to accommodate new business development needs and methods.

The following is an anecdote often used to explain paradigms:

> You erect a pillar in the middle of a room with a high ceiling. You then leave a bunch of bananas at the top of the pillar and bring five monkeys into the room. One of them soon discovers the bananas and starts climbing the pillar to get to it. As it climbs, you hose it down to prevent its ascent. As the others attempt to climb, you also knock each of them down in the same way. Some of the monkeys try five or six times, but none of them reaches the bananas at the top. In time, something interesting happens: they stop trying to get to the bananas. This means that they have learned something from their experience. However, the experiment is not yet over.

> You replace one of the monkeys with a new one. The newcomer soon spies the bananas at the top of pillar and starts climbing, but other four try to stop him. Even though he doesn't know why he's being pulled down from the pillar by the others, he eventually quits trying, because the force of the others is too strong to resist.

> After a while, you again replace one of the monkeys with a new one. This new monkey starts go-

ing after the bananas at the top of the pillar. The rise of this one is also stopped by the rest of the monkeys, including the one that was introduced a short time before.

After one monkey after another is replaced five times in succession, no monkeys in the room have experienced the forceful water of the hose. Now you replace yet another one. The attempts by the new monkey to get at the bananas are restrained by all the other monkeys.

The following exchange sums up why the animals have stopped trying:

A: Why stop me?
B: I don't know, but I do know that this has been the course of action here for some time.

This is the way the paradigm works. There is a tacit understanding among the monkeys that they should *not* do things a certain way.

2-2. Defense mechanisms

Taga also appear in the form of defense mechanisms, which have been studied extensively in the field of psychology. People employ these techniques to protect themselves when they feel vulnerable or threatened in a certain situation. Because all human beings are prone to them, these mechanisms emerge from time to time. They are unlikely to emerge when people are working in isolation, but they surface when people are working or interacting in a group, such as a meeting where issues are being discussed. When this taga emerges, it often prevents people from thinking and acting positively.

Say, for example, you're in a meeting and you want to propose as many good ideas as possible, hoping to win the attention and respect of your peers. But what might happen if you're unable to come up with the number of ideas or proposals you had hoped for? You might remain positive and say to yourself, "All right, I didn't come up with many good ideas this time, so I'll just listen to what others have to say and give my opinion where possible." On the other hand, if you unconsciously refuse to accept yourself for not being able to generate many ideas, a defense mechanism will emerge to protect yourself. You may become negative and start complaining.

Studies on defense mechanisms have a long history and are defined and categorized in many ways. However, from our experience we believe that they can be divided into three main mechanisms.

1. Hostility. This mechanism also manifests as defensiveness or criticalness. It becomes manifest in people when they refuse to take responsibility for the way they are and blame some person or thing. They see their true selves as different from their present selves and don't accept the way they are. For example, if at a meeting they can't come up with enough ideas, they blame the facilitator or the way the meeting was conducted. In our Innovative Thinking System™ training

in Japan, we see this defensive type most often in people at a senior level or in a higher age group.

Here's a good description of what we might see during our training in Japan: People from a senior level or a higher age group may think something like "I'm the oldest participant, so I need to act as a leader for the group." As the training begins, the trainer starts to present an array of techniques and methods, one after the other. However, the senior-level participants often have difficulties quickly grasping what's being said. While the younger participants move ahead with many ideas in exercises on techniques, the senior participants tend to fall behind. When the time comes to present their ideas before the group, they may feel that their presentations are off the mark. They may even get some suggestions from younger participants on how to improve their presentations. They're likely to grow discouraged due to anxiety because of their lack of understanding, so this defense mechanism emerges at least once or twice in the course of the training.

If these members could just accept the fact that they're slower in understanding, it wouldn't be such a problem, but they can't and, as a result, become defensive. When it's time for their afternoon coffee break, they might stop one of the trainers and engage in an exchange like the following:

A: Let me ask you a question. Is this program just a rehash of something developed in the United States?
B: Yes, it is, to some extent.

A: Well, that's no good. It won't work in Japan.
B: Why not?
A: I can tell. It just won't work.

Having said this, he or she continues grumbling.

In other cases when people become defensive, they might complain about our method of teaching, or they might become indignant and tell us that we need to give them more time to think, that what we demand of them is unreasonable. It's understandable that some people take longer than others to understand, but these people don't want to admit it. These reactions are typical of a "hostile" defense mechanism.

2. Withdrawal. Those who resort to this mechanism often use it as an excuse for failure before they even try to perform a task. People who withdraw have high ideals, but they run out of steam at the very thought of the effort needed to achieve their goals. We see this sort of behavior very often at our training sessions as well. Although these people may start out with a positive attitude, when they find that they aren't able to generate as many ideas as others in a group, they withdraw from further participation.

The typical pattern of behavior of these people is to offer one idea, write it down, and then do nothing else for the rest of the session. They just sit with their arms crossed and look out the window or up at the ceiling. When the trainers try to encourage further efforts by suggesting they try to come up with more ideas within the time allowed, they're apt to respond by saying,

"This is good enough. I'm not really very serious about this." When we hear a response like this, we might feel compelled to respond by saying, "Well, how about getting very serious then?" The fact is that these people don't want to be in a position where they may have to acknowledge inferior performance, should they make an earnest effort and not succeed. This is the psychology of people who want to avoid failure at all costs.

3. *Indifference*. People who resort to this type of self-defense neither make excuses for being incompetent nor act hostile toward others. They simply remain aloof, passive, or unresponsive to what's going on around them. They may show some effort in the beginning but will become defensive when the situation turns unfavorable to them. Typically, these people stop talking to others or ask to be left alone.

In our training, we often have an indifferent person announce something like this: "I just want to let you know that I'm here only because I was told to attend by my boss. He said we have to attend seminars, and it happened to be my turn, so I'm here even though this has nothing to do with my work. I don't want to interfere with what all of you are trying to do here today, so please just carry on."

After this declaration, the person may actually start to isolate physically from the group—by moving his or her chair away from the table, for example. This defense mechanism is to protect himself or herself by pretending to be indifferent.

The above are specific examples of the three main types of defense mechanisms. All people on occasion resort to the use of defense mechanisms to some extent to try to protect themselves, and they resort to different mechanisms according to the situation. Irrespective of the type of mechanism, the person under its influence stops thinking positively once the mechanism is at work. Understanding this, we may be able to realize that when we stop thinking positively, it may be an indication that we are being defensive.

The late Dr. Will Schutz taught us that people demonstrate signs of defensiveness before they actually move to protect themselves. He refers to these as "clues to defensive behavior" (2008, 76). If we're able to detect any of these so-called clues, we should be able to prevent any interference in our ability to think positively. Here is a list of the signs noted by Schutz:

- Loss of humor
- Taking offense
- High charge or energy in the body
- Sudden drop in IQ
- Wanting to be right ("No question about it")
- Wanting the last word (rise in volume of voice)
- Flooding with information to prove a point
- Endless explaining and rationalizing
- Playing "poor me"
- Teaching or preaching
- Rigidity
- Denial
- Withdrawal into deadly silence
- Cynicism (victim)

- Sarcasm
- Making fun of others (being highly critical)
- Terminal uniqueness
- "It's just my personality; it's just how I am"
- Don't want to negotiate
- Blaming
- Sudden onset of illness or accident
- Confusion
- Suddenly tired or sleepy
- Intellectualizing
- Acting crazy (the temporary insanity defense)
- Avoiding discussions
- Being too nice
- Selective deafness (hearing only what I want to hear)
- Attack (the best defense is a good offense)
- Holding a grudge
- Trivializing with humor
- Inappropriate laughter or giggling
- Yelling
- "I'm aware of that; leave me alone" (defense of awareness)
- Addiction to alcohol, drugs, people, shopping, working, gambling, chocolate, training programs, etc.

3. Three ways to fend off defensiveness in the workplace

Productivity in a meeting will be low when defense mechanisms are at work among participants. This will be the case particularly at meetings convened to generate new ideas. Few people realize that defensiveness can be fended off with a small amount of effort simply by taking a few precautionary measures. Below are some examples of such measures.

1. Make the workplace atmosphere creative and open. How can you create such an atmosphere? Brainstorming might be helpful. One of the most widely used methods for promoting thinking "out of the box," this concept was developed by Alex F. Osborn in 1953, almost sixty years ago. When Osborn was running an advertising agency, he found that it was easy to generate a wealth of ideas at meetings simply by following the four basic rules below (Osborn 1963, 155-58).

Rule 1: Never be critical, judgmental, or find fault with other people's ideas. In creativity development, the two terms *divergent* and *convergent* are often used. To diverge means to branch out in various directions, while to converge means to hone in and narrow down ideas to bring them close to their final form. Osborn insisted that no one was to criticize or find fault with any of the ideas people presented during the diverging process in creativity development.

At many meetings convened to generate ideas, however, we witnessed people immediately making comments or finding fault with ideas the moment they were presented. Consequently, meetings of this nature tended to end with the proposal of only a few ideas, even after a lengthy session. According to Osborn, a critical review and discussion of ideas should be reserved for the convergent process.

Before the start of a brainstorming session, it's essential that this rule is clear to everyone. Note, however, that this rule does not restrict participants from asking for clarification or explanation of an idea they don't understand. Therefore, at the start of a session, this rule should be explicitly stated: *We will have no comments or criticism of the ideas at this stage.*

Rule 2: Invite everyone to present with total abandon as many ideas as possible. At this time, ban the use of disparaging words such as *ridiculous* or *stupid*. During sessions where we were observers, we occasionally witnessed individuals become irate at another's contribution and make disparaging comments. Once a person becomes the target of this form of censure, he or she will usually refrain from making remarks or sharing an opinion again. So here is the explicit rule: *Please feel free to present any thoughts or ideas, even if you think they're farfetched or outrageous. Who knows? These may become the source of inspiration.*

Rule 3: Connect and expand on the ideas. The objective here is to invite participants to add to and further elaborate on each other's ideas. Ideas of one participant may evoke interesting associations or inspire new ideas in other participants. The facilitator's job here is to keep the ideas flowing, growing, and expanding—*not* to direct the discussion in one particular way or another. A facilitator that insists on controlling the meeting will be unsuccessful in creating a free and open atmosphere. Instead, the meeting will become claustrophobic, and generating ideas will become a laborious task. In such a meeting, a dialogue like the following is likely to take place:

A: So, Mr. Yamada, what do you think?
B: Nothing in particular.
A: How about you, Mr. Sato?
C: I don't have any particular opinion either.
A: Mr. Suzuki?
D: Me neither.
A: I see. Let's go on to the next idea then...

This type of dialogue only contributes to a stifling atmosphere.

Rule 4: Aim at generating ideas in large quantities. The objective is to come up with as many ideas as possible. The more ideas you can craft, the more alluring the possibilities become. If at this meeting you need to reach a conclusion, it would be good to spend the first half of the meeting generating as many ideas as possible and the second half narrowing them down.

If the above four rules are made clear to everyone before the meeting begins, the atmosphere will be free and open, and participants will be unlikely to adopt a defensive attitude.

2. Make the workplace atmosphere receptive and positive. The worst reaction a person can experience is rejection. When we're told our ideas or proposals aren't good enough or are uninteresting, we certainly won't want to speak up again. The second worst reaction a person can receive is no reaction at all from the other party. This also becomes a cause of anxiety. Whatever the idea or proposal, it's important to be receptive and positive in our response to others.

Some ways of showing we're receptive to others in the course of an exchange or discussion are to nod in agreement or to interject brief comments as we listen, such as "I see., "I understand," "Yes." People feel more at ease and willing to speak and more willing to participate in a discussion when they feel what they have to say is accepted and valued.

So the meeting facilitator must help set the tone of a discussion and atmosphere of a meeting by being receptive and positive. There may be times when we can't help but think the idea being proposed is absurd, but acknowledging it rather than rejecting it can make all the difference in the workplace environment. A critical assessment of the ideas will take place later during the converging process anyway, so it's more productive to devote our energy and time to generating ideas at this diverging stage.

3. Make the workplace atmosphere attentive and supportive. It's not unusual for people at meetings to present their ideas in a manner that isn't well thought through. Instead of telling the presenter to come back when he's more organized, it would be more constructive if you first listened carefully to what he had to say and to give support by trying to rephrase or confirm in your own words the ideas you believe he is trying to express.

Some useful interjections might be "So, I think this is what you're saying. Am I correct?" or "In other words, your idea is to…" If the presenter agrees, a likely response from him might be "Yes, that's exactly what I was trying to say." Responding in this manner makes people feel that what they're saying is acknowledged and valued. Creating an atmosphere like this also fends off defensive tendencies and enhances the productivity of meetings.

Yet many managers create an atmosphere at meetings that is the exact opposite. These managers are good at directing the flow of proceedings on their own terms, telling attendants to refrain from making irrelevant remarks and then dominating the discussion themselves. They have a tendency to reject people's opinions categorically and point out their faults, and they have a habit of interrupting discussions that are underway and turning antagonistic. Consequently, those in attendance become defensive or unwilling to participate further. The result is an unproductive meeting that ends in a tense atmosphere.

Fending off defensiveness in people is not that difficult. Knowing that defensive forces are at work in people sometimes is all it takes, and this knowledge is sure to make your meetings much more productive.

In this chapter, we learned about several forces that influence innovation, about taga as obstructions to innovation efforts, and about how to avoid defensiveness. In part one, we referred to some authorities to help us understand the importance of innovation and taga that might be obstacles to innovation efforts. In part two, we'll look at methodologies for promoting innovation efforts.

PART II

METHODOLOGIES
FOR INNOVATION

CHAPTER 4

SEVEN WAYS TO GENERATE IDEAS

In this chapter, let's now look at ways to craft innovative ideas. Following are idea-generation techniques to help make innovation take place, and they constitute the first part of our Innovative Thinking System™ program. Here we'll focus on how to incubate ideas. These techniques are applicable to both product innovation and process innovation. (Look at the left side of figure 3 as a reference for this chapter.)

Figure-3: Construct of the Innovative Thinking System™

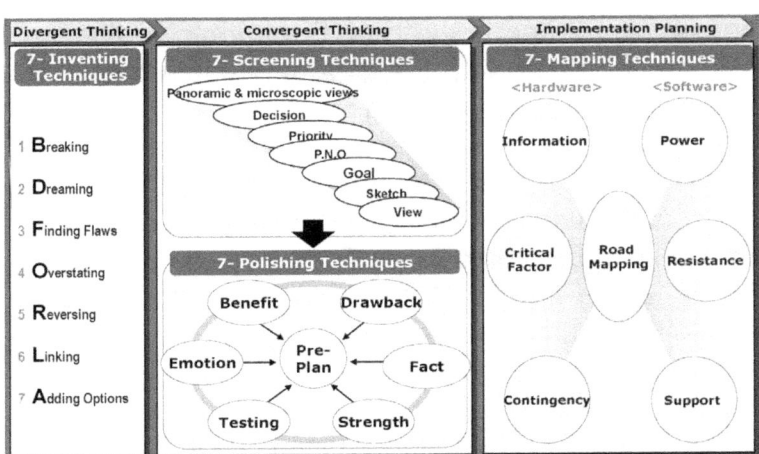

1. Think in a trajectory that moves away from common sense

People often use the expression "think outside the box." But at work, our minds are fully occupied with thinking firmly "inside the box." We're absorbed by thoughts of our workplace, the business we engage in, our firm, our products and services, and the way we go about our work. So we have to begin by freeing our minds from the things that occupy them.

The first step is to write a list of things that come to mind when we hear the term *common sense*. The second step is to see what kind of ideas we can come up with by breaking outside the bounds of common sense.

Take, for example, the SILENT Piano™ of musical-instrument maker Yamaha—a good example of thinking outside the box. The notion that musical instruments are created to produce sound is, of course, common sense, or thinking in the box. Going outside the box, Yamaha came up with the idea of an instrument that, when played, could be heard only by the player through a headset. This product was naturally a major success in Japan, because it matched the needs of Japanese consumers who live in relatively small houses in close proximity to their neighbors. Following the success of the SILENT Piano™, Yamaha came out with a series of silent instruments based on the same concept—silent violins and silent cellos—and these significantly boosted their profits. The idea further led them to introduce acoustic guitars, light-guided guitars, and even guitars that play on their own without plucking the strings or pressing on the frets.

Another example of thinking outside the box is Prudential Life Insurance's "life benefit policy," which pays benefits to policyholders for the remaining period of their life when they're diagnosed with a terminal illness. This concept is the exact opposite of conventional life insurance policies, where premiums are paid throughout life, and benefits are received only at death. This policy covers up to 80 percent of the insured amount and is paid to the policyholder upon the issue of a doctor's certificate verifying that the life expectancy of the insured is, for example, only a few months to less than a year. This policy concept was well received in the market, and became a major force in the firm's ability to win a large share of the life insurance market.

Just imagine what you could do with the money that you would never have received otherwise. Say that you had a policy worth half a million dollars. At an 80-percent payout, you would receive 400,000 dollars. While you're still healthy enough, you could go visit those places you wanted to see before you die. You could buy presents for those you love and those who have supported or looked after you. Incidentally, Japan's regulatory authority initially didn't approve this policy concept, because it was not genuine insurance; it was way outside the box of convention.

The above are just a few examples of the kinds of ideas that can be incubated by breaking away from common sense or usual practice. What new ideas for products and services could your company come up with by throwing common sense out the window?

2. "Dreaming"—Indulge in fantasies of what could be

Under normal circumstances, we think in practical terms of how things should be based on experience and the facts of life as we see them. If we happen to come up with something out of the ordinary, people are likely to react by saying, "Are you dreaming? Be realistic!" Science and technology are firmly rooted in facts and reality, but many concepts of science and technology had their beginnings in wishes and fantasies that were realized only after much thought over a long period. Dreams to fly made airplanes come true, and the desire to move around under water at will resulted in submarines. These are good examples of ideas incubated from indulging in fantasies.

When you need to generate a good idea, allow yourself to step away from reality for a moment and think, *What are all the possibilities? How can it be done?* From there, begin to entertain every idea about how you'll get there.

Fumiaki Funada, a former engineer at Sharp, was once asked, "What attracted you to liquid crystal research?" He replied, "I wanted to make a wall-mounted TV." This is a well-known anecdote in Japan. That was more than thirty years ago. And, as they say, the rest is history.

Many people today can't imagine life without computers. But twenty or thirty years ago, computers were bulky, very expensive machines, and they were used by only a select few experts in specialized fields of study, such as orbital calculation. Today computers are small, inexpensive, high-performing, almost ubiquitous household items that people use for a multitude of purposes, including family bookkeeping, accessing information on the Internet, and communicating with friends. Indeed, the potential uses of computers seem to be almost unlimited.

In the early days, computers ran on very complex programming languages. Remember COBAL and Fortran? Back then, we had to spend hours and hours of our time learning those technical languages in order to run those early machines. Naturally, we wished for simple instructions to give to computers. Today we have personal computers that just about anyone can run. Now computers even have voice-activated and voice-controlled functions, which are good news for those of us who are disabled or sensitive to mechanical or electronic devices.

If you want to incubate ideas for a business, product, service, design, or system, go after imaginative, fanciful ideas, and decide how you can give them form with the know-how and technology available to you. Be deliberately greedy when broadening your wish list, and don't allow critical comments like "That's absurd" or "This doesn't make sense" to seep into your thinking. Continue by writing down your ideas or drawing pictures or outlines of how you can get closer to the object or idea you wish for.

3. "Finding Flaws"—Identify flaws and faults

The idea here is to focus attention on flaws or faults that cause inconvenience or dissatisfaction in a given situation. This exercise in problem solving is often used by companies in Japan where they apply QC or QC circle activities. This approach is widely applied in new-product and service development.

Let's consider improving services or systems at a supermarket. First, think of aspects of shopping that shoppers might find inconvenient. For example, if they shop in the early evening, they may have to wait in a long line at a checkout counter. Next, think of what could be done to resolve the situation. Obviously, the idea would be to avoid congestion from occurring at the checkout counter. So now you have to think of ways to achieve this. How about a system for counting items by shopping basket or cart with the use of a magnetic device or laser? Or you could imagine a system or aisle for all purchases to be settled by debit or credit card only, instead of cash. Or payment for specific items could be made in the sections where they are sold instead of paying for all items at checkout counters. What's important in this task is to hone in on the issue of inconvenience and identify it in specific, concrete terms that encompass the who, when, and how of the situation.

4. "Overstating"— Expand or reduce

This is a classic approach to new-product develop-ment or a project. For example, the challenge may be to reduce something that's the size of a desktop to a palm-sized object. Or the challenge may be to en-large the object to the extreme. The former, "miniatur-izing," is an area where the Japanese have excelled, and many specific examples can be cited.

Nobuyuki Idei, a former audio/video unit chief at Sony, often used this approach. He was in the habit of ask-ing his engineers to "reduce it to this size" and indi-cating the scale in dimensions technologically unfea-sible to anyone. He would then go on to demand that the engineers achieve the impossible by telling them, "This is your mission," and leaving them to wrack their brains for ways to get even close to the target size. This was how he pressed them to come up with as many innovative ideas as possible.

An example at the other end of the scale is Aurora Vision, a mammoth TV screen installed at a stadium. Mitsubishi Electric Corporation developed it as the re-sult of a project to create a screen that fifty thousand viewers could watch at one time.

The above examples of enlarging and reducing are two extremes, but this concept can be applied in vari-ous areas, not only in dimensions of physical size. For example, President Masayoshi Son of Softbank Corporation, a mobile telecommunications provider, prepared a three-hundred-year vision for his company, an extremely lengthy, unconventional time span that became a topic of conversation. Whatever the case, the idea of expanding or shrinking things to extremes stimulates inspiration in our thinking.

5. "Reversing"—Think in opposites

When we consider objects or matters, we can think of them in terms of dichotomies, or opposites. Some examples are "optimistic and pessimistic," "quantitative and qualitative," "heads and tails," "plus and minus," "direct and indirect," and "simple and complex." Being able to think in terms of opposites is an important mental technique for visualizing and constructing ideas in the abstract. When we conceive of an idea in the abstract, we can also reverse it from front to back, top to bottom, hard to soft, or light to dark.

We've found that many flexible thinkers tend to think in contrasts. This is what we mean by reversing or switching. Even though on occasion it's just a stroke of luck that a product becomes extraordinarily popular, it's often said that hit products come from thinking in opposites. The point here is to be mindful of applying this as another technique for expanding your thinking.

The "bathroom dryer" concept by Panasonic Electric Works—meant to make a wet bathroom dry—is a good example of ideas developed from considering opposites.

Another interesting story about incubating ideas from this concept is that of the popular Dakara, a mineral drink developed by Suntory. It's an isotonic drink containing minerals and other ingredients. Suntory had retreated from the mineral drink sector of the market once, and a project team was formed to find a way to reenter the market, which was already crowded with competitors. The team's task was to come up with ideas for products that would differentiate Suntory's products from those of competitors.

No good ideas seemed to surface, even after meetings and discussions for many months. At last, one good product concept happened to emerge. Exhausted at work late one night, the project team members decided to call it quits for the day and to take a moment to relax in a sauna on the way home. Just before entering the sauna, the team leader asked out loud, "Why do we gulp so much water right before sweating it out again?" The reply from a member was "If we drink a lot of water before a sauna, we sweat more, and it's good for the body."

A new drink concept came like a flash to the leader's mind. *Yes, we need to replenish what has been lost from the body.* His concept emerged from an idea that was the reverse of drinking, that is, the body discharges what is taken in. This ended in a health drink that supposedly promotes the discharge of excess fat, salt, and sugar. Its unique TV commercial of a little boy urinating— a Manneken Pis lookalike—was also launched from this conceptual viewpoint.

6. "Linking"—Connect disparate ideas

Synectics, a word derived from the Greek word meaning "hold together," is a method of identifying and solving problems by joining unrelated elements to one another. The idea behind this approach is *serendipity*, a word that means "to get lucky by chance." It happens to be a very popular concept in research and development units of firms. English author Horace Walpole supposedly coined the word from Serendip, an old name for Sri Lanka. He explained that this name was part of the title of a fairy tale called *The Three Princes of Serendip*. In the story, as the three princes traveled from place to place, they continually made discoveries, by chance and good fortune, of things they were not even searching for. Walpole coined the name as many discoveries and new inventions in the world of science and technology were related to events made possible by chance. Following are a few examples of such serendipity.

First is the story of DuPont in the 1920s. At that time, DuPont was trying to diversify by developing new products. Gunpowder and explosives were its core products. In the process of researching the possibilities of creating products from polymers, a research assistant happened to forget to turn off a burner one Saturday. On the following Monday, he found that the polymer that had been exposed to the flame all weekend had condensed into fibriform. Further research on fibriform led to the development of a new material called nylon. This discovery made DuPont one of the largest textile companies in the world. In Japan, it's well known that Toray Industries, a Japanese firm capitalized at only seven million dollars, paid DuPont ten million dollars in royalties for nylon. Thanks to nylon, Toray grew to become a blue-chip firm.

Next is the story of 3M. In the early 1980s, an engineer named Spencer Silver was researching a strong adhesive. Despite his efforts, he failed to get the right blend of ingredients and ended up with a rather weak one. Yet he found out that this adhesive maintained its stickiness even when it was removed from objects it was adhered to, though it wasn't very strong. Silver told his colleague Art Fry about the adhesive. Fry regularly went to church on Sundays and was a singer in the choir. The bookmarks he used to hold places in his hymnal had an annoying habit of falling out of their places as he turned the pages. He decided to try the adhesive Silver had told him about and was pleasantly surprised to find that, even after removing and replacing the bookmarks a number of times, they maintained their adhesiveness. This was the beginning of Post-it® notes, which are now sold all over the world, reaping millions of dollars in profits for 3M.

We also have a serendipity story from Japan to share. Let's go back to Sharp, where Fumiaki Funada was conducting research on liquid crystal with his boss, Tomio Wada. They were working with pure liquid crystal but faced an uphill battle in finding a practical use for it, because it took too long to transform from a liquid to a solid state. One day Mr. Funada left the lab without replacing the cap on the container that stored the pure liquid crystal. When he showed up at work the next day, he was shocked at the discovery of his blunder. He thought this would bring his research to an end. The pure liquid crystal, which is extremely expensive, had become contaminated with impurities. Though disappointed and dejected, he decided to perform one last experiment before discarding it. Much to his surprise, the solid chemical reaction this time was much improved. This "contamination" turned out to be significant in the progress of his research.

All of the above are stories of serendipity that people are fond of telling. Yet they aren't stories of luck alone. In each case, the people did much to exploit the serendipity, including ongoing efforts, keen observation, clear intentions, and perseverance. The lesson here is that serendipity isn't to be viewed as a lucky gift of chance but as an approach to be used purposefully when trying to give form to ideas and concepts. Synectics is a method used to make serendipity occur. It involves taking random thoughts, mixing them together, and then linking them to see what new ideas can be drawn from them.

7. "Adding Options"— Clarify your direction

All of the six ways to give shape to an idea thus far are approaches that challenge us to see phenomena from different angles and perspectives. But there's one more method we use that's aimed at squeezing out one or more ideas from a proposition, if possible. This method involves slicing or cutting into the proposition to see it from various cross-sectional perspectives. This essentially means expansively and exhaustively exploring one idea and then adding options and applications. In other words, this step is to stay within one theme of a subject topic and to see if there might be options or alternatives.

This is one technique for thinking of approaches to a theme based on information, knowledge, and experience. At this stage, rather than twenty or thirty ideas, your possibilities will be much more promising if you have two hundred to three hundred ideas to work with. The important point is to include every single idea that comes to mind, no matter how ordinary you think it is. From among these ideas, you may be able to draw a good idea. Even if you can't, you may be able to "combine" one or more of these with a proposal that's presented in the next stage.

It's very important to understand that in many cases, the most wonderful ideas in the world are often combinations of a number of very ordinary ideas. That's why it's better to have a large number of ideas to consider in combinations. However, rather than blindly stating ideas, it's more efficient to try to give ideas in an organized manner in a short time. This will help clarify the direction and the "cuts" to be made. Again, examples can explain this step better. For example, think of the uses of a small vial. Stay within the range of liquids, rather than exhaustively exploring all possible uses. So the vial could be used for soy sauce, oil, vinegar, a spice, or another seasoning.

For cuts, or facets, relating to upright vessels for holding things, some possible ideas are a vase for holding flowers, an umbrella stand, or a pencil holder. In this way of thinking, we can generate a lot of ideas faster, easier, and in a well-organized manner. This is a basic concept of this approach.

Following are examples of cuts applied when discussing measures or plans for taking on business issues that we're more familiar with. If we just discuss the ideas in a conventional way, we seldom come up with many ideas compared to the amount of time we spend. However, if we have some of following cuts, it might be much easier to generate many ideas in a well-organized way. First, prepare the cuts and then add ideas according to them.

Issue:	*Cut:*
Plans for products and services	Quality, product and service lines, brand, warrantees, distinctive features, and utilities
Research and development	Patents, technology, personnel, external networks
Financials	Cash flow, long- and short-term borrowing, control methodologies, and tools
Costs and outlays	Overall outlay, costs by department or unit, costs owed to suppliers
Sales channels or marketing	Distribution, dealer sales capabilities, sales promotion expertise, distribution management know-how, salesforce support, servicing capabilities

Production	Procurement capabilities, production know-how, costs, facilities

Other cut examples of business plans are corporate image, personnel, organization management know-how, group companies' capabilities, public relations, and promotions. These are just some examples from which many ideas can be drawn.

Again, the point of this method is to increase the number of options or alternatives in a specific subject by starting from sectional cuts or cross sections. Typically, we all have a tendency to expect to find an excellent idea from the very beginning of idea generation. But we seldom have such a lucky break. If we keep searching for choices or options, even simple ones, excellent ideas may emerge from a previously unnoticed "blind spot." If not, the ideas can be mixed or combined to come up with more choices or options.

We've reviewed seven ways to generate many ideas. In the following chapter, we'll look at the next step for innovation efforts: selecting appropriate ideas from among many. Our thought process will be totally different than this chapter described.

CHAPTER 5

SEVEN WAYS TO NARROW DOWN IDEAS

We've assisted various corporations and organizations with change and innovation based on our fundamental concept that innovation is a combination of creativity and practice. Therefore, it makes sense that the results a company achieves depend on the extent to which it practices product innovation and process innovation. So, to continue with processes and practice, the next aspect we'll look at is how to choose from among many ideas, groom them, and plan their implementation. As we do this, the question we must consider is, What can we do to raise the success rate of ideas that have already been proposed? Following are a few important points.

The first task is to narrow down the many ideas to a few. Whatever theme we consider, we generally come up with plenty of ideas, so the first step is to select a number of ideas that could be put into practice. In this step, you should choose from among these either as individuals or as a group, selecting the ideas from a subjective viewpoint in terms of their adequacy, relevance, and validity. You won't know if the ideas are adequate, relevant, or valid from an objective view-point unless you try them all.

In reality, the number of ideas that could be selected for implementation won't be many, since most firms have limited management resources, including personnel, budget, and time. So you want to select ideas that appear to be convincing. Now, let's look at some of the techniques for narrowing down a large number of ideas. (For your reference, see the upper center of figure 3, "7-Screening Techniques" on page 69.)

1. Bird's-eye and bug's-eye screening

When you're trying to narrow a list of ideas to those that you feel are valid and convincing to the group, try to appeal to people's five senses. This is done in two ways: panoramic viewing (bird's eye) and microscopic viewing (bug's eye).

During panoramic viewing, write down each idea on an index card or Post-it® note, and spread them all on a table, the floor, or a wall. Then allow enough time for everyone to go around and familiarize himself or herself with each and every idea. This is bird's-eye viewing.

Next, sort or group the cards or ideas that have a commonality or relation to one another. Then give a name or title to each idea group, and closely examine each idea to choose the best idea in the group. This step is bug's-eye viewing. The final step is to bring together all the best ideas from all of the groups to settle on the final idea for a specific subject.

The final idea may be your solution, or a combination of a number of final ideas may be appropriate. Whatever the case, narrowing down ideas in these steps should encourage people in the group to participate and feel more positive about the idea selection.

2. "Decision" screening—Narrow down according to the reason for selection by individuals

This is a technique for taking individual decisions to the group-decision stage smoothly. When Innovative Thinking System™ techniques are applied, it's common to see groups sometimes produce one thousand, two thousand, or even more ideas. But how can this number be effectively reduced to a few final ideas that are acceptable to the group? Here are a few steps to follow.

First, set aside enough time to review all ideas presented by the group. Ask each member of the group to select four or five ideas that he or she thinks are good ideas. Ask group members also to provide—in as much detail as possible—their reasons for selecting each idea.

Second, have the members individually present their choices and write them in a list as they're presented. Alongside the ideas, list the members' reasons for selecting the ideas. At this point, even if there is no overlap and there are five people in the group, the maximum number of ideas would be twenty-five; but generally, there is some overlap.

Third, discuss the reasons for selecting the ideas and their importance. Rank the reasons in order of importance before selecting the top five. If there are five or six reasons on which the members agree, have them look at the idea list one more time and score the ideas based on their importance (five or six agreed-upon reasons). For example, devise a scoring system in which the most important ideas— based on the reasons—are given a score of five and the second most important a score of three, etc. Now compare the points on ideas given by each member of the group. Ideas in order of importance should be clear by now, because everyone in the group can see them in numbers. If the points don't clarify the order, score again for only those ideas getting points. From our experience, this will help to clarify the order.

Because these steps allow everyone in the group a chance to evaluate the importance or priority of ideas, this is an effective way to narrow down ideas.

3. "Priority" screening—Prioritize according to assessment criteria

Perhaps evaluating ideas based on criteria is the most popular method of narrowing down the number of ideas. The following are some examples of evaluation riteria.

Appeal of the idea	Predicted market potential
Effectiveness	Steady demand level
Feasibility	Added value
Novelty value	Consistency in corporate image
Capability in technology	PR merits
Market appetites	Time horizon in market introduction
Problem-solving capability	Relevancy to the current market
Relevance to technology	Competitiveness
Investment risk	Effectiveness in promoting on employment opportunities
Market maturity Intensity of competition	Contribution to business momentum

The standards you choose will vary depending on the subject or topic you're considering, but the four that can be applied most easily when ideas are being assessed by individuals or a group are appeal, effectiveness, feasibility, and novelty.

It's necessary to discuss carefully what evaluation criteria you will use, because they will determine the order of priority. Once standards are set, however, each idea will be evaluated according to those standards. For example, if you're judging the appeal of the ideas, you may give scores from one to five, indicating the level of their appeal. Evaluate each idea on a number of standards, and decide on the ideas of top priority based on the idea with the highest number of total points. You can then group the ideas into a first-priority idea group, a second-priority idea group, and so forth.

Keep in mind that the group needs to reach a consensus on how many points to allocate to each of the criteria. Naturally, people will have different views. Some people may give five points to feasibility, while some others only two points. When this happens, don't be in a rush to rule by majority or take the average number of points of the group. Rather, try to reach the total number of points by discussing among the group the rationale for the points given. Otherwise, there will be a lingering feeling of dissatisfaction, making people less willing to participate further.

One way to make the weighing of points more understandable would be to define or to try to articulate what five points in profitability would mean as a standard and what four points would mean. You need to determine what weight you'll give to the criteria themselves. For example, novelty value may be weighted three times more than other standards by one firm, while profitability at another firm may be weighted two times more, and applicability of the current technology at yet another firm may be weighted threefold.

Research and development units at most firms carry out exercises like these. We've helped develop these standards for many clients. In most cases, the method of weighing standards to standards is confidential, so we can't give specific examples here. On the other hand, it might be an interesting exercise for you to devise a set of standards to suit your own organization.

4. "PNO" screening—Judge by comparing Positives (merits), Negatives (demerits), and Originality (uniqueness)

We usually feel attracted to ideas that are long on merits but short on demerits and things that are one of a kind. So the method this time is to highlight the distinctive, conspicuous features of each idea as well as its merits and demerits, put them in a list, and compare them. *Distinctive* here means something we instantly feel when we hear or know of an idea.

This method is not only simple and easy to use, but also convincing as a method of narrowing down ideas. Consider, for example, sorting out ideas for designing a new personnel system. One of the ideas may be an honor system for the monthly salary, in which employees submit statements of the amount they should be paid. What might be its distinctive merits, benefits, advantages, or upsides? One of them may be that high-performing staff can ask for higher pay. On the other hand, what may its demerits, faults, or draw-backs be? It may be that payroll costs would soar.

Next, list the unique aspects of this idea. One might be that the idea is interesting since everyone gets to know who asks for what pay or since we get to know people's personalities or characters through what they ask for. Finally, compare all ideas on the list. This makes it easy for everyone to come to an agreement and decide on the best idea.

5. "Goal" screening—Review in light of primary objectives and aspirations

At some point during the process of narrowing down ideas, pause for a moment to revisit the initial idea objectives. This approach validates and clearly re-confirms the objectives so that they lead you to select appropriate ideas.

Every firm has specific objectives in searching for new business ideas. One firm, for example, might need ideas for the second or third main lines of business, since the core lines are not doing well. Or, at another firm, such as a low-key industrial materials supplier where the core lines are doing well, the chief executive has given a directive to the project team to search for new business ideas that will enhance the visibility of the firm. The team then needs to define ideas from the standpoint of how much recognition or visibility the firm is seeking. For instance, one firm in Japan bought a profes-sional baseball team as a new business. In another example, a firm's plan might be to shut down two of its plants in the next three years, though this has not yet been announced to the public. The president of the firm has asked a special team to come up with a new business idea that will create four hundred jobs for the employees of the plants to be closed. He says that any line of business will be okay, as long as it doesn't go into the red. So the team's task is to narrow its focus to businesses that can employ four hundred people but that will not go into the red.

As the examples above illustrate, objectives and goals of firms for new business ideas are all company-specific. So the approach here is to define or clarify the motives, intentions, and goals of the idea objectives repeatedly when narrowing down ideas.

6. "Sketch" screening—Review by comparison with the rough plan

This approach can be used when narrowing down ideas for undertakings that require a significant amount of capital outlay, effort, people, facilities, equipment, and/or technology.

The first step is to define—in terms of what and how—everything required for the idea to go forward. Next, plot the resource requirements in a rough, chronological sketch indicating, for example, the early, middle, and late stages. This process makes it possible to clarify which resources and how much of each is needed.

Write down how many people you may need and if it will be possible to engage that number, as well as how much money you will need and whether it can be budgeted. The same goes for the facilities, equipment, technology, and so forth. Do this for each of the ideas you are considering.

Then move on to a discussion in which you compare ideas to determine which idea or ideas are most practical and feasible. This approach might tell you that you will need 250 people altogether for the first idea, but only fifty people for the second idea and one hundred for the third. And then, if you can transfer seventy people from your plant, the second idea appears to be the best as far as the number of people goes.

7. "View" screening—From a management perspective

This approach is effective in narrowing down ideas when approval of a board or managing directors' committee is required for an idea to move forward.

Lay all ideas on the table, and discuss each one in turn by asking the following questions:

- To what extent is this idea aligned with the firm's management philosophy, principles, and values?
- Is the current business/market environment interested in this idea or against it?

- Is this idea feasible in terms of the firm's resources in people, facilities, equipment, capital, and available technology?
- Is this idea in accord with the firm's business objectives or fields?
- Does this idea coincide with management plans?
- Can this idea be molded into a story or vision that the senior executives are telling?

If the answers to these questions appear appropriate, the idea is likely to win the approval of people at senior level. Try to see which one of the seven approaches we have discussed above works best for your organization.

In this chapter, you learned how to screen ideas and select appropriate ones from seven different angles. In the next chapter, you'll find hints for fine-tuning selected ideas to develop a proposal to get approval for idea implementation.

CHAPTER 6

SEVEN WAYS TO REFINE IDEAS

The next stage for enhancing the possibilities of success through practice is grooming and refining your ideas. No particular method, approach, or discussion is required if the idea doesn't need the consent or cooperation of other people. But even in those cases, it's good to have a framework for your idea to increase the possibilities of its success. And in any organization, that case would be rare. You'll come to a hurdle or gate where you must win approval from your superiors or support from colleagues for your idea to move forward.

The chance of your idea's success increases when people fully understand and support it. Therefore, you need the right tools to communicate with them. A proposal that communicate clearly is even more important when you need to enlist external support or cooperation for your idea. This chapter will show you how to firm up your ideas and bring them closer to their final form as a proposal. Following are seven useful approaches. (See the lower center of figure 3, "7-Polishing Techniques" on page 69, for your reference.)

1. "Emotion"—Refine your ideas based on people's reactions

If an idea is unanimously supported by all parties involved, it will certainly be approved and will receive the cooperation of all. In reality, such cases are rare. This is why it's very important to be attentive to how other people might react to your ideas. For instance, which people or department might not like your ideas? Next, consider how you can smooth over or dispel those feelings. Somehow you have to clarify the issues.

Ideas have an effect on people's feelings. It's important to remember that the first impression tends to be a lasting impression. So if people's first impression is negative and those feelings are not dealt with, they're likely to point out your ideas' faults in a very logical way. Therefore, it's always important to find and be ready with ways to assuage people's negative feelings when you make a proposal.

2. "Benefit"—Refine your ideas in light of their benefits

What do you think will encourage people to approve and support your ideas? Certainly, they need to see some merit or benefit in them. The more benefits they see, the more attracted to the ideas they are apt to become. Understanding this, make efforts to identify and emphasize as many benefits as possible.

You must also be clear in your expression of your ideas so that the image you're trying to convey appears clearly before their eyes. Try to list and emphasize any and all benefits, and dress them up in the best way you can. Your confidence in and enthusiasm for your idea will also increase through this process.

3. "Drawback"—Refine your ideas in light of their drawbacks

Any idea also has shortcomings; it would be extraordinary to have an idea with no disadvantages whatsoever. Therefore, you need to identify and overcome shortcomings to present your idea in the best possible light. We sometimes hear about "failed" ideas, which flounder when disadvantages and negative aspects emerge when they're subjected to the scrutiny of others. These ideas are destined to fail as proposals.

It's natural for people to try to find fault with a proposal when they're presented with its positive aspects only. Their motivation to find negative aspects increases the more the benefits are emphasized. Some likely reactions include "What you say may be true, but what about this?" and "Don't you see this as a disadvantage?" Senior managers, who usually think in logical terms and speak from experience, often raise negative points.

Preempt negative reactions and doubts by promptly responding, "Yes, we are aware of this, and we intend to handle it like this." This will likely elicit positive reactions and support from managers. You can't come up with a solution for all disadvantages ahead of time, but do your best to be ready to respond to negative feedback. If you are well prepared, your proposal is much more likely to be acknowledged as realistic.

4. "Facts"—Refine your ideas with facts and figures

Every idea needs to be backed up with confirmed facts and other relevant information. For example, if your proposal involves technology, check the status of patents. If you're getting ready to propose a promotional event or advertising campaign, investigate applicable laws and regulations beforehand. Failure to investigate and confirm essential information and figures can result in unexpected difficulties when you put your idea into practice. For example, you get the go-ahead to proceed with planning that includes budgeting, development, and all the attendant resource requirements, but then your plan hits the wall due to a patent issue. Imagine how devastating and wasteful that would be. Imagine the huge drain on resources and human effort.

At any rate, it's best to confirm facts and figures before moving forward with a proposal. In most cases, fact finding and confirming conditions are the first steps in actioning a plan. So refine your ideas in light of those steps.

5. "Strength"—Refine your ideas by upgrading initiatives

Make every effort to enhance the appeal of your ideas. One way to do this is to add other ideas to remove any anticipated obstacles to implementation, to simplify the original idea so that anyone can understand it easily or to highlight the appealing aspects. Hone only those ideas aligned to the set objectives. For instance, when you're trying to cut costs, a new idea should not add costs. Don't kill the goose that lays the golden egg. When you and your team members refine ideas together, make sure everyone keeps this in mind.

6. "Testing"—Refine your ideas based on testing

Sometimes approval of an idea is hard to come by when the idea proposal requires a significant amount of human resources, capital outlay, facility resources, or high-level technology, all of which come with risks. The higher the risk, the more difficult it is to get top management to give approval. In this case, consider proposing to conduct preliminary testing of the idea along with your original idea proposal. Testing can help alleviate concerns regarding uncertainties. And approval will be more likely, even if your original idea proposal is declined because of the risk. If the testing goes well, top management might reconsider your original idea.

7. "Pre-Plan"—Refine your ideas

It is time to translate your idea into a proposal. There are many different formats for a proposal, depending on what the proposal is for. Is it for a new business project, a new product or service, or a new system or structure design? Once the objectives of the proposal are clear to you, you can organize ideas and form them into a plan proposal. Following is a list of items to consider when drafting a proposal.

Subject title of the idea proposal

Fee structure/payment schedule

Synopsis

Supplementary services

Description text

Advertising/publicity

Illustrations

Promotional event

Outline

Advertising campaign

System drawings

Alliances

Flow charts

Partnering

Motives/intentions

Circulars/flyers

Market/business environments,

Product/service potentials conditions

Objectives/goals

Market potential

Advantages/impact/ effects/outcomes

Materials purchasing/ procurement

Sales turnover potential

Logistics

Sales/profits projections

Production/ manufacturing/assembly

Benefits/advantages to the firm	R&D
Related/associated effects, affects	Costs
Required number of personnel	Distribution/outlet channels
Project team organization charts	Concerns
Promotional support/ backing	Issues
Target market/customers	Measures/ countermeasures
Projected images/icons/ representation	Simulation/testing
Intended specs	Missing information/ confirmation
Required technologies/ availability potentials	Study/survey subjects, items
Customer acquisition methodologies	Subject items to be confirmed
Key/cornerstone points to success Pricing	Plan development schedule/timetable

If you review the above topics as you make your plan, you'll likely end up with a very realistic, practical plan. But one point of caution: avoid compiling a lengthy plan for your presentation. If you have only ten minutes to present your plan at a board meeting, you won't be able to cover everything in a thirty-page document, and the board members will probably skip over parts of it. In many cases, one or two pages are enough. Preparing yourself ahead of time by reviewing every pertinent point in your proposal will increase your confidence in the presentation.

However, new initiatives usually involve a high level of uncertainty. You may not be able to access or obtain all the information you require, and you may not be able to remain confident about your plan. This is why you need to be ready with facts and evidence to support your plan. A board member might ask, "What is your projection on this factor on the first page of your presentation?" Even though you may not have clear ideas on projections because this is a new initiative, your response shouldn't be, "I'm sorry. I don't have any." That might draw an automatic rejection. Instead, offer an answer that shows you have given the subject some thought. When you're asked a question like "What are your grounds or reasons for this on page two?" you can respond by saying something like "The evidence is clearly stated and verified in this supplemental handout. I can give you a copy." Saying this gives you a far better chance of receiving approval. These responses will make the board members recognize that your proposal is well thought out and that you are confident in it.

In this chapter, we reviewed some ways to refine and polish your idea and make an effective proposal. The key is to focus on several ways to make your idea more attractive and realistic and to make your proposal more likely to be adopted.

After successful adoption of your idea, you'll move to the next step: developing an action plan for your idea implementation. In the following chapter, you'll learn what to focus on as you develop it.

CHAPTER 7

SEVEN MAPS FOR IMPLEMENTING IDEAS

After your idea proposal is adopted, you should develop a successful road map—in other words, an action plan—for putting your idea into practice. It's also important to share the action plan with the members of your idea implementation team.

In this chapter, our discussion moves on to specific actions that can help take an idea to the next level: its implementation. To increase the chances of your ideas being successful, use the following guidelines, or maps, in a methodological and systematic fashion. (See a picture on the right in figure 3, "7-Mapping Techniques" on page 69 for your reference.)

1. Collecting information—Map an action plan for collecting information

Most ideas start with some kind of information-collecting activity. When these processes and methods aren't clear to you and other members of your idea implementation team, your chances of success decline.

How do you define information? According to Claude E. Shannon, information reduces uncertainties or unpredictables in the decision-making process (Shannon 1948, 623-56). For example, think about casting a die. The chances of coming up with the number one is one out of six. However, what if you're told that the die that you cast has been doctored and will come up with only odd numbers? You know that the chance of the number one turning up is now one out of three. That is, the odds are twice as good, meaning that uncertainties have been halved. In the same way, collecting information is a process of reducing or clarifying uncertain and unpredictable elements. The more you clarify uncertainties, the easier it is to make decisions in the implementation process.

Helping the group (you and the other members) gather and collect information requires more than simply telling others to go get information. If you do this, they'll come back with low-quality information. It's unlikely that sort of information will reduce uncertainties, which is the objective. Clearly lay out who will gather what information, where, by when, and on what level.

The next task is to clarify the extent of the information required. One simple method is to classify the types of information required into three levels. Information at the top level is must-have information. Without this information, the plan can't move forward. Basically, information at this level may be all the information you need. Information at the second level is "desirable" information, which complements or supplements the must-have information. The third level is information that would be nice to have, if it can be obtained. Classifying information into these levels is particularly important when many people in the group take part in this task, either on their own or collectively. This makes it possible to gather targeted information that's high in quality and that will help reduce uncertainties.

There are two types of information: information in print or data (secondary information) and information obtained firsthand in the field or from individuals (primary information). Secondary information is found in documents or electronic sources, such as the Internet. Primary information is obtained only by going to the source or by having someone in the group go to the source to gather the information. One notable difference is that secondary information gives you the impression of knowing primary information, which is not the same as knowing it. In other words, information in print and data is helpful and important, but remember that it may not always show you the facts.

Here's an example. If you're planning to go on an overseas trip, you can get all sorts of information about a certain hotel on the Internet. But if you have friends who have already been there, they can give you useful, firsthand information that you may not be able to find elsewhere. For example, they might tell you, "The restaurant at the hotel was always so crowded that we couldn't eat there." In the same way, collecting information from primary sources should be a priority when working on your information map.

2. Protocoling—Map an action plan for critical factors and tasks

The second map for enhancing your project's chances of success is clarifying key processes and actions to take. Most ideas and plans encounter critical junctures and stages. If the steps and procedures at each of these key points or stages aren't clear, the chances of success dwindle. Eliminating any ambiguity or any unclear areas in steps to be taken is essential.

Having this map is especially important when many people are involved in different steps at the same time or must carry out the same task individually yet simultaneously. If, for example, the task of your team is to go out individually and purchase a parcel of real estate in different areas of the country, the procedures on purchasing need to be clear to everyone and followed uniformly, so when the task has been completed, no one is left lamenting, "I should have checked with everyone beforehand."

Having this map is also beneficial when certain jobs are more or less the same and are to be performed again and again. Opening new distributor offices in different regions or giving the same kind of presentations to different audiences are two examples of this. If you have such critical processes in your idea implementation, having this map for them will increase your project's chances of success.

3. Planning for contingencies—Map an action plan for contingencies

The third map for enhancing the success of your idea project is to have contingency measures and items to be actioned in your idea implementation. Most projects or plans are exposed to risk in one way or another. Consider some worst-case scenarios: you have a technical problem or a contract with another firm is canceled or one of your distributors goes bankrupt. To brace for such problems, you need to have a contingency plan in place to prevent or minimize damages. It's never too early to predict, plan ahead, and have an action plan on hand for any possible event. A good contingency plan can enhance the success of your idea.

Unexpected events do happen. But if an action plan is in place to deal with high-risk, potential events that would have a significant impact on business, there's a strong possibility that you can respond to the situation promptly and smoothly.

It's impossible to plan for every unforeseeable event, but disaster readiness is essential. Planning for emergencies strengthens your plan, which will increase its likelihood of success. It also puts you in a strong position for responding to disasters should they occur.

4. Influencing and affecting—Map an action plan for utilizing powers

The fourth map for boosting the chances of your idea's success is setting out how to influence people involved in the plan. Provide a definite strategy about whose support you will need and how to go about obtaining it, so that your plan will move ahead as scheduled. Normally, most people in an organization have heavy workloads and do not have the luxury of providing you with help just because you ask.

So, how do you influence people to help? Max Weber, who pioneered the analytical method in sociology, was the first person to analyze in a systematic way the power of people to influence others. He pioneered a path toward understanding how authority is legitimized and proposed a theory of authority centered on three types: traditional, legal-rational, and charismatic. Along the same lines of Weber's ideas is the theory of the "seven power bases" proposed by Hersey, Blanchard, and Johnson (2008, 163-66). Here we will apply these in drawing up a map for influencing people.

1. Exploit "coercive power." This is "the perceived ability to provide sanctions, punishment, or consequences for not performing." Try to conceive of how you can exploit coercive power to move your idea project forward smoothly. Sometimes alarm or scare tactics can be effective.

2. Mobilize "connection power." This is "the perceived association of the leader with influential persons in the organization." Try to examine how to make use of your own and others' personal connections. Normally, people are more willing to offer support to those they feel close to or familiar with, and are less apt to turn down a request. Mobilize all connections and net-working power.

3. Apply "reward power." This is "the perceived ability to provide things that people would like to have." People are generally willing to offer support if they believe they will get something in return. In addition to financial rewards and promotions, consider intangibles such as positive feedback or encouragement on a job well done. While some people shun the idea of offering a carrot, rewards still talk. It matters not only that rewards are offered but also that they're perceived as rewards by those who receive them. An effective tactic is to find out what kinds of rewards appeal to the people who will receive them.

4. Leverage "legitimate power." This is "the perception that it is appropriate for the leader to make decisions because of his title, role, or position in the organization." Consider how to leverage someone's position or title. It's much more effective to ask for people's cooperation with a letter of endorsement from a senior executive than with a letter of endorsement from a unit manager. Use others' power as leverage.

5. Tap into "referent power." This is "the perceived attractiveness of interacting with the leader." Referent power comes from people's personal traits, such as integrity, fairness, and honesty. Encouragement, admiration, confidence, trust, and rapport are a few of the important attributes necessary for affecting people. You may have a case where it would be effective to ask respected people for help to encourage

someone to be on your side to move your project forward.

6. *Utilize "information power."* This is "the perceived access to, or possession of, useful information." In general, people within a company are generous and willing to offer support to others who give any kind of helpful information to them. People may feel that they may not be able to receive any information if they refuse to give support to you if you are an information source. You should think of how to use this power to move your project forward effectively.

7. *Take advantage of "expert power."* This power is "the perception that the leader has relevant education, experience, and expertise." How can you take advantage of others' expertise? Generally, follow the advice or guidance of experts when they tell you that you must do things a certain way. When you work on part of a plan that's unfamiliar to you, ask for the assistance of experts. You have power behind you if you are able to say that you were instructed by experts to take a certain course of action. Or, if you are an expert in an area, you can utilize this power for successful implementation of your project.

Now let's move on to the fifth map.

5. Negotiating with people—Map an action plan for important negotiation

The fifth map for increasing your project's chances of success is to clarify how and what to do when negotiating, conferring, and liaising with others. Most ideas involve some form of negotiating. So, what negotiating needs to be done for your project to move forward, and how should it be done? This map allows you to proceed with successful negotiations, which we would never advise you to leave to chance.

Here it's crucial to map an action plan thoroughly and vigorously for each step of negotiations, which should be in line with established terms and conditions as much as possible. It will also make a big difference if you can offer compromises. Be ready with tactics as you lead your negotiations with the other party, with a goal of finding common ground.

Imagine yourself at the time of negotiations with the other party. How much thought have you given to the conditions you will adhere to and the concessions and trade-offs you are willing to make to get what you want? To enhance your chances of success in your project negotiations, be ready to clarify intentions, conditions, and areas of compromise. It's also important to share this map with your project members so that everyone—the team as a whole—is clear about the points in important negotiations with other party.

6. Boosting support—Map an action plan for getting support from others

This next map involves clearly considering how to secure others' support. First, enlist the support that you'd like to have from others. Your requests for support will progressively decline on people's priority list unless you define ahead of time the specific activities or items you need from them. Also, your project's chances of success are slim unless you have a definite action plan for maintaining their cooperation. Being inattentive about activities that maintain good relationships will also result in people becoming psychologically distant from your project. The dialogues below illustrate this problem.

> Junior employee (in the planning department): Is our earlier request about the plan going well?
> Manager (in the sales department): Sorry, we can't afford to do anything about that now, since we have three sales promotion events going on at the same time. Can you wait a little bit longer until things quiet down?
> Junior employee: We can't do that. As you know, the plan was approved by the board. If we don't move ahead with it, we'll all be in trouble.
> Manager: I understand, I understand. I will get on it.

Does the manager really mean to give instructions to his colleagues about the plan? It's more likely that he's growing uneasy about the junior employee not showing sympathy for or an understanding of how busy the sales department is and thus will be unwilling to take the plan seriously any time soon. Wouldn't it be better for the junior employee to ask for support a little differently?

> Junior employee: Is our earlier request about the plan going well?

Manager: Sorry, we can't afford to do anything about that now, since we have three sales promotion events going on at the same time. Can you wait a little bit longer until things get quiet down?

Junior employee: I see. I actually heard from my colleagues about how busy the sales department is, with so many events going on. So I'm sorry to have to bother you about the plan. I have an idea, though. Can we younger staff at the planning department help with the events in any way? We want to contribute to the events as well as sales as much as we can. If my colleagues and I can go visit clients, I think we can also start working on the plan. Can you please let us know what you think?

This is much more positive in tone and in spirit. The manager is more likely to be motivated and encouraged to respond by saying, "We have to move on this plan soon."

It's essential to have a dedicated action plan focused on how to get key people and groups involved, while being attentive to their feelings, situations, and reactions. This will enhance the chances of your plan's success.

7. Defining member roles—Map an action plan in detail

The last map for enhancing the chances of your project's success is defining the roles of the people involved in the project. Many projects require clear guidelines about the roles people will play and clear statements about the duties that accompany those roles. Your project will be much more effective if it includes specific descriptions of each task, who will carry them out, and when they should be completed. The plan should also state when and how adjustments or corrections are to be made if activities fall behind schedule, as well as who is responsible for checking that aspect of the project. Clarification of these areas will significantly facilitate the practical management of the project.

In project management practice, it's important to note what is called "the first 10 percent rule" as a means of risk control, emphasizing the importance of catching early warning signs in any project (Shibao 1999, 78-79). One study showed that all projects that were behind schedule at around the 20 percent completion stage (the entire project phase was considered 100 percent) ultimately finished more than 10 percent behind schedule.

This highlights how important detailed planning is, including checking any deviation from initial plans before a project progresses beyond the 20 percent stage. It's crucial to study the detailed action plan to determine how those involved in the project are performing, including those in charge of adjusting and correcting the schedule.

Using these seven maps will increase the chances that your project will succeed. The crucial point in all these efforts is never to leave room for miscommunication with the people involved.

In chapters four through seven, we learned ways to generate ideas, screen and polish them, and develop an action plan for successful implementation. In the following chapter, we'll introduce some applications of this concept in Japan.

CHAPTER 8

CASE STUDY: INNOVATION MEETINGS

After more than fifteen year of experience practicing the Innovative Thinking System™ program with our client organizations, the following approach is the one that we feel the most enthusiastic about. It's the Innovation Meeting, an approach that contributes directly to corporate innovation efforts.

We've introduced this approach to a diverse array of firms and organizations, including a large communications equipment supplier, a sanitary equipment supplier, an academic institution, a toy and game producer, a confectionary manufacturer, a pharmaceuticals firm, and an auto maker, to name a few. This meeting approach has helped produce many benefits and results in these companies in areas such as new products and services, boosting their revenue and profit, productivity, cost reduction, employee satisfaction, and corporate recognition and reputation. The typical procedures are mentioned below.

Our clients' most fundamental motive for introducing the Innovation Meeting to their organizations is to reap the benefits gained from Innovative Thinking System™ program training. Standard training is delivered in a four-day program; more in-depth training is conducted over six days' and the shortest course is a minimum of three days. After trainees complete their training, they're eager to apply it, not just in a training environment but, more importantly, in the development of products and services and in process innovation. Almost immediately after their training, they reconvene to continue their discussion on methods to improve their practices, propose ideas, and refine them to determine their implementation potential.

A meeting usually runs for two to three days and is attended by a group selected from the trainee graduates. The meeting generally starts with an opening message accompanied by a pep talk from a director from research and development or an executive-level meeting organizer. The message and talk generally includes an overview of the firm's position in the market, the mid- to long-term landscape and outlook, the importance of the meeting, the scope of ideas to be parsed, the surrounding conditions, and the provision of relevant information.

The remarks also include a statement of the objectives and expectations of the meeting, along with the procedures and the treatment and processing of ideas and proposals that come out of the meeting. The discussion phase begins, and each group with at least one leader starts to pump out innovation ideas for about two-thirds of the entire session. If it's a three-day meeting, this part will take two days. If it's a two-day meeting, it will take about a day and a half.

The remaining one-third of the time is spent sorting and organizing ideas into a top-priority idea group, the second priority idea group, and "all others" idea group. During the second part of this phase of the meeting, participants groom the overall concepts of selected ideas in the first group and shape them into a detailed plan proposal. In the concluding part of the meeting, a progress report is presented along with further discussions and a question-and-answer session.

A typical meeting with twenty participants generates about eight hundred ideas. These will be narrowed down to about eighty concepts in a rough format, and about twenty detailed idea proposals will be drawn up. A subsequent checking and screening meeting held after a few more meetings often picks up ideas missed at the narrowing-down process.

When this meeting is held five times, there will be somewhere around four thousand ideas, which are narrowed down to four hundred concepts in a rough form. Close to one hundred detailed idea proposals are then developed. Some time ago, an R&D chief of a firm complained that his staff was already generating a lot of ideas, but very few of them were any good. When we asked how many that was, he replied two hundred or so a year. This number doesn't even compare to the numbers that come out of an Innovation Meeting.

In most cases, the roster in a meeting is made up of three or four people from various units or departments. Knowledge of Innovative Thinking System™ (ITS) techniques is a prerequisite. A typical composition of a meeting is staff from component technology, technology development, R&D, production technology, budgeting, information control and administration, patent and intellectual property, sales and sales planning, and marketing and promotion. This representation draws on the "onlookers seeing more than the players" effect. A bystander's vantage point inspires free-floating ideas and questions, such as "Can this be possible?" "Can that be done in this way?" This promotes the development of the plan proposal and is a significant point in a meeting. For example, comments or observations of people outside the R&D box may make people inside the R&D box aware of a blind spot.

A meeting is also intended to draw wisdom, good judgment, and insight in an organization to a maximum level. It also supports a decision-making process at a top executive level. It's a good idea to ask executives to observe a meeting for half a day or so, which also works as a motivation to participants. An even better approach is to have a few executives not only observe but also respond to report presentations with their thoughts and express their desire to check on the progress of the plan proposals in the future. In general, this kind of meeting is concluded by a leader announcing the next step in the executive review schedule.

Afterward, the group holds a few "perfecting meetings" to hone the plan proposals selected. Meanwhile, all ideas in a rough outline are filed for further reference, if necessary. All proposals from perfected ideas—say, about one hundred of them—are drawn onto flip charts for detailed examination and assessment by the board. The assessment meeting starts with presentations by each subgroup given simultaneously in the morning. Board members split up to examine the presentations for each subgroup's presentation, along with the same assessment checklist. In the afternoon, twenty or so proposal finals are subjected to further scrutiny and evaluation by the board before a vote is taken, a budget allocated, and a project plan drafted.

Plenty of new projects have been developed in our Innovation Meetings. In many cases, projects have made a new-product introduction to the market and commercialization, resulting in a sales and profit boost at our client firms.

CHAPTER 9

CASE STUDY 2: A METHOD APPROACH TAKEN AT A HIGH SCHOOL

Although we have applied the Innovative Thinking System™ (ITS) here for innovation in business, it can also be applied in other organizations, such as schools, colleges, nonprofit organizations, and government offices and agencies.

One case in point is a private high school in Japan that has practiced this method and used ITS as part of the student curriculum. The school had been one of our client organizations for many years for seminar presentations and various training programs. In 1997, we introduced a three-day Innovative Thinking System™ program to the faculty members and staff as part of their training program to enhance creativity. In the following year, the program was offered to its group schools as a tool for exploring new business possibilities. New initiatives drafted at that time later significantly contributed to organization innovation at the high school.

At about this time, one of the administrative officers came up with an idea to embed the ITS program in the high school curriculum. A project team determines whether and how this might be possible. First, we conducted trainer development programs for faculty and staff members, and within three years, the entire faculty became certified trainers. In addition, the project team of faculty, together with our team, offered the students pilot program training and finally developed a program text for high school students. While we had extensive experience in providing ITS training for many hundreds of firms, this version of the program for high school education was very new and worthwhile to us. So it can be said that this program has developed into a form of academic-business cooperation.

Incidentally, the school's initial goal in introducing this program was to apply integrated study (integrated learning periods) elements being advocated by the then Ministry of Education. Integrated study was an initiative aimed at remedying force-fed education and cramming practices in Japan by designing new approaches to learning. These aspirations were enshrined in the School Education Act. As it turned out, the ITS training at the high school attracted a lot of attention and was covered in economic dailies, TV, magazines, and other media.

While we now have over two hundred officially certified trainers of ITS practicing mostly at corporate organizations, the Innovation Meetings mentioned above and the initiatives taken by the high school are, in a way, something of a new chapter in ITS training.

Today we often hear people comment that Japan as a whole has been losing its competitive edge in the world marketplace for the last ten years or so. Japan, a country of diligent, industrious people who have demonstrated unrelenting efforts, a persevering spirit, and enthusiasm, once stood at the forefront of almost all industrial sectors in the world. Whether it can regain the momentum it lost and again play a leadership role in industry and technology in the next ten years could very well depend on how robustly it can reinstitute its innovative thinking on a nationwide scale.

In chapter eight and nine, we introduced two case studies that show the application of the Innovative Thinking System™. The situations could be different from or similar to your country. In addition, the information may be applicable to you or may not even be understandable in your situation. However, we hope you've found something helpful to you and your organization.

PART III

MINDSET FOR SUPPORTING INNOVATION

In part two, "Methodologies for Innovation," we discussed some practical approaches and methodologies to assist in promoting innovation. Part three covers some other subjects pertinent to learning, creativity, and innovation. To deepen your understanding of change and innovation programs, we'll also share more of our experiences from working with many hundreds of client organizations.

CHAPTER 10

LEARNING PRODUCTIVITY

So far, we've touched on the importance of learning about change and the mechanism of innovation, and we've learned about various methodologies. In this part, we look at what happens to people when efforts at innovation become an integral part of the organization as a whole.

What, then, are the elements related to productivity improvement in learning? First is the interest or appeal of the subject matter. When the subject is appealing and relevant to our work, we become interested and engaged, and our learning productivity goes up. If we believe the subject matter has nothing to do with our work, we can't get interested, we fail to engage with the content, and our learning productivity falls.

Second, it depends on the extent to which the subject matter to be learned coincides with the learner's ability to understand the subject. People get motivated to learn more when they feel they can understand what they're supposed to learn, but they stop making efforts when they feel this is not the case. This means that the greater the gap between the learner's ability and the difficulty of the subject matter, the further the learning productivity will decline.

Third, productivity improvement in learning depends on how urgent mastering the subject matter is for your work. For example, what would you do if you were told of a new assignment that would require you to spend at least two years in a foreign country where a language you don't know is spoken and that your assignment there begins in six months? Perhaps you would try your very best to learn the language, either by going to a school or hiring a personal tutor. Either way, you would make an earnest and serious effort. You might think that you should first become accustomed to work and life in your new setting and try to learn the language through practice rather than study. But you feel uneasy about this, since you need to concentrate on your work as soon as you get there. Under these circumstances, you would be motivated to make an all-out effort to learn the language.

As you can imagine, learning productivity changes significantly depending on how crucial you feel the subject matter is to your needs. Conversely, productivity doesn't increase if, for example, people have the attitude that a certain method of training is for people in R&D but not for them in the accounting and finance unit, even though they're told that the training is for innovation. Well, it comes down to the proverbial question "Which comes first, the chicken or the egg." Without compelling reasons, learning productivity will not increase. "Pressing need" is the very driving force of innovation.

Other aspects affect learning productivity. For instance, health is a factor. The productivity of people who suffer from poor health can be expected to decline. The productivity of people with extremely heavy workloads will also be impaired, because concerns over their work and about not being in a position to learn wholly absorb them. Anxieties and worries in people's personal lives also lower their productivity.

However, these aspects of lower productivity are not as serious as the three main aspects discussed earlier. After all is said and done, kindling compelling needs toward innovation in the daily activities of every staff member is the key to raising learning productivity in an organization.

In the following chapter, we'll focus more on the mental aspect.

CHAPTER 11

SELF-ESTEEM

Dr. Will Schutz, one of the most prominent psychologists and practitioners of interpersonal relations and personal development of his time, wrote about self-esteem in his famous work *The Human Element* (2008, 19): "Self-esteem is the core of each person, the center from which all creativity, motivation, and productive work issue." We all need to have strong self-esteem if we are to perform well and are to demonstrate our abilities to the fullest.

If we don't understand this fundamental theory, we can't discuss organizational change or innovation. Promoting change and innovation in an organization is sometimes accompanied by the risk of losing your status in the organization to some extent, or at least you may feel so at a subconscious level.

Let's stop to think for a moment. Suppose you decide to propose a new plan to the organization and are ready to act on it. Do you think there is any new proposal that comes without risk? Whether consciously or otherwise, you would certainly start weighing the potential risks and their extent. If you felt that the risks would be too great, you would stop pursuing your plan. But a major factor that comes into play in your decision making is your self-esteem.

Schutz analyzed self-esteem from three perspectives (2008, 65, 89). The first is people's feelings of self-significance—how important they as individuals feel in the organization or the unit they belong to as well as the importance of the work they perform or the role they play. Some people feel that they're performing such important work in the organization that if they don't show up for work, the work in their unit will grind to a halt. On the other hand, some feel that the work they do isn't worthwhile and that if they took a leave of absence for a month, it wouldn't affect the flow of work. Most people in a company stand somewhere between these two extremes.

Now, which of these two types of people do you think will be forthcoming with new proposals? Of course, it will be those with strong sense of self-significance. People with this strong sense reason that since they play an important role in the organization, they ought to be active in suggesting ways to make the organization better. On the other hand, people with a weak sense of self-significance may tell themselves that because they don't play an important role, their ideas won't be of any worth, even when in fact they may be. The distance between these two types of people is huge in terms of their efforts. Since feelings of self-worth aren't always evident to others, other people may feel that a certain person is very important to the company, even when that person doesn't feel that way.

Schutz's second factor in self-esteem is the feeling of self-competence. This is the measure of how capable we feel in terms of the work we perform and the roles we play within our unit or the organization. While some people feel that they're quite capable in almost every area of their work, including solving just about any of problems that arise, others feel that they're limited in skills and overall competence and not good at problems that surface. Again, most people fall somewhere between the two extremes.

So, which of the two types do you think would be more forthcoming in making new proposals? Without a doubt, the people with a strong sense of competence will be more willing to make proposals. They reason that since they're competent, they ought to be active in proposing new ideas to help make the organization better. The people with a weak sense of self-competence will be reluctant to share their ideas, even when they are good ones, because they see themselves as having poor skills and questionable competence. They may also feel uneasy if a proposal they put forward is accepted and they're asked to take charge of it. They may lack sufficient confidence and worry that even a good plan could fail if it's entrusted to them. Again, the distance between these two is enormous in terms of efforts. Again, since feelings of self-competence are an internal part of our makeup, other people may perceive a person as being highly competent even when the person does not.

Schutz's third factor of self-esteem is the feeling of self-likability. This is a measure of how individuals see themselves as being well liked by their colleagues in their unit or in the organization as a whole. While some people feel they are cared for, not only in their department but also by all people they have dealings with at work, some people aren't so positive and may feel that they aren't well liked by people either in their own unit or in other departments. They may feel this way because of the reactions, feedback, responses, or expression of others. In this case, too, most people fall somewhere between the two extremes.

Which type of person do you think would be more willing to make new idea proposals? To be sure, people who feel they are well liked will be more actively involved in making propositions. They may make proposals without any hesitation, because they feel confident of other people's feelings toward them and have little fear of falling out of favor with their colleagues or friends because of their actions. Rather, they may feel at liberty and confident to say just about anything they might have on their mind. On the other hand, people who don't feel well liked rarely put forward a proposal, even when they have a good idea, because they fear that the possible rejection of their idea could lead to being disliked even more.

Once again, since feelings of this nature aren't always evident in people's expressions, a person who is actually well regarded by colleagues may feel the opposite.

Self-esteem is the combination of people's feelings of significance, competence, and likability. People have varying degrees of confidence in all three areas, and while some may feel very secure about themselves, others do not. To create an organization that autonomously promotes change and innovation, it's necessary to increase the self-esteem of the people in that organization. The people of the organization are the ones who propose and implement change. Unless they have sufficiently high self-esteem, they will be unable to take initiatives or lead innovation. In other words, sustained innovation can't take place in an organization made up of people with low self-esteem. Again, people have self-esteem, and we need to have deeper understanding of the concept of self-esteem as innovation leaders in an organization.

If you would like to know more about this subject, we recommend that you read Schutz's *The Human Element*. We believe that creativity and self-esteem are the operating system software of an organization. No matter how sophisticated your computer may be, it will never function at its maximum potential when the operating system is obsolete or malfunctioning.

We looked at the importance of self-esteem in this chapter. In the following chapter, we'll look further at key blocks to creativity in innovation that we've learned both from Schutz and from our experiences in Japan.

CHAPTER 12

BLOCKS IN THE CREATIVE PROCESS: INSECURITY

Schutz practiced training and offered consultation to people for many years to elevate self-esteem at a number of well-known firms. When we asked him once in a training session about the creative process, he told us that a fear or a sense of conflict in people blocks creativity (2008, 164-67). The question is, what might these insecurities be? Following are what we understand to be the insecurities among people in Japan, based on Schutz's definition of blocks in the creative process.

1. Fear of not being creative

Most people have doubts about their creativity at one time or another. Some may doubt that their ideas are creative enough to please their bosses. And some may never think of themselves in terms of being creative at all, so they never come up with even one idea that they feel is worth sharing. When people are full of anxiety and uncertainty about their own creativity, their creative thought process naturally becomes blocked.

2. Fear of lacking rationality

Every person wants to be rational. And when we share ideas with people, we need to do it logically. At times, however, we fear that we're either lacking in logic or overemphasizing rationality. Most discussions and tasks in an organization are done in a logical manner, and the reaction we want to hear from others is "I see" or "That makes sense." In other words, people want what is reasonable.

Nevertheless, when we're trying to start something new and creative, it may not be possible to explain each and every attempt rationally or logically. Many undertakings make sense only when we put them into practice. Sometimes intuition brings new discoveries. But people remain wary of giving the impression to others that they're illogical. Regardless of the extent of those fears, when people are uncertain about their logic, their creative thought processes are stymied.

3. Fear of humiliation and embarrassment

People often worry that they will be told, "Is this the best you can come up with?" Unless they have unshakable confidence in their ideas, they worry about making a fool of themselves. When this anxiety is strong, their creative thought processes are compromised.

4. Conflict over being ignored

People also become concerned that their proposals may not be taken up at all. When they feel that they aren't valued as people, they become diffident when proposing ideas. For instance, your humiliation would be even worse if someone made you feel like "You aren't even in a position to make that kind of proposal." You would feel that there was no place to hide at your workplace. Even the possibility of having others look down on them can make people shy away from offering ideas.

5. Fear of rejection

Propositions may be rejected outright and explicitly. The risk of being rejected increases further when a proposal is somewhat outside the range of what's considered practical, feasible, or possible. Even if they know there's some chance of being rejected, people fear the unpleasantness of an outright denial.

6. Anxiety over not being appreciated

All members of an organization care how they're appraised and wish to receive approval and be valued. They wonder, How will making this proposal affect the way I'm regarded? If it's approved, will I be valued more? And if it isn't, will people regard me less? Worrying about how others appraise them also disrupts people's creative thought processes.

7. Fear of failure

Every idea carries a risk of failure. As discussed earlier, an innovative organization has a culture that tolerates failure and the unexpected. In reality, however, most organizations aren't that forgiving or lenient toward failed attempts. That said, nobody could ever be 100 percent certain that a proposal will result in a successful outcome. Nevertheless, when fear of failure is excessive, it only serves to suffocate creative thought processes.

8. Lack of rewards

Normally, people are willing to try harder when they can expect a reward in return. Conversely, if they feel that there's no reward at the end of their efforts, they're likely to lose motivation for putting forward proposals that will come to naught.

The items listed above are what Schutz analyzes as people's feelings of insecurity that block their creative thought processes. Which feelings of fear would you perceive or suffer from most? Pause to make a list. If they are identified, you may be able to overcome fears or anxieties that otherwise would not have been removed.

CHAPTER 13

TEN PSYCHOLOGICAL FACTORS IN RESISTANCE TO INNOVATION

At a seminar presentation in Japan (1975), Dr. Gordon Lippitt, a well-known behavioral psychologist and professor emeritus at George Washington University, stated that people often buck how change takes place rather than the change itself. Below are some of the reasons he gave for people resisting when an organization attempts to institute change. His thought is helpful especially when you implement ideas for reducing resistance from others.

1. Unclear goals

People resist when the purpose of innovation is unclear. Attempts at innovation meet with opposition and are likely to end in failure unless the organization gives clear answers to questions about why innovation is needed and what the organization hopes to achieve through innovation.

2. Inadequate involvement in change

People are likely to oppose change when they feel change efforts are being made only with a select group. They may be frustrated by the lack of involvement in changes that are going to affect them and refuse to be cooperative under these circumstances. Plans executed in this manner rarely go smoothly.

3. Insufficient communication about change

People resist change when they're informed of it only in the most perfunctory way. When they're suddenly told about imminent changes out of the blue, they're alarmed and wonder when the decision regarding the changes was made and why they weren't informed sooner. Resistance under these circumstances occurs frequently in organizations; people are more likely to resist change when they feel left out of the loop.

4. Based on personal appeal

People become suspicious and immediately wonder who is going to benefit from the change. They may even rebel when they feel that the only ones benefiting are those who are pushing for the change. They may grow frustrated or even protest by questioning why they should get behind efforts that are for the benefit of others. A plan that gets started on this track is headed for major problems.

5. Inadequate rewards

When people see the rewards of their efforts as inadequate, they resist even when the change or innovation is successful. People aren't willing to devote efforts to initiatives they perceive as having little benefits.

6. Fear of the unknown and fear of failure

People become negative about their own initiatives if they suddenly feel anxious that they might run into trouble if they attempt something no one has ever been successful with before or if the attempt fails. The more anxiety people feel, the more they resist.

7. Satisfaction with status quo

When people are satisfied with the status quo, they're likely to resist change. That's because change involves risk, and they don't want to compromise their favorable situation by introducing change. The more people feel uncertain, the more they resist change.

8. Ignoring group norms

Any organization, unit, or group is bound by norms, a term in behavioral science defined as an established standard of behavior shared by members of a group to which each member is expected to conform. Irrespective of whether the values on which the norms are based are "good" or "bad," there's an implicit understanding and tacit consent about work rules and other matters.

For example, consider "this is the way it's done here." In this case, it's better to do it that way. When you ask why everyone shows up at work by eight o'clock, even when working hours don't start until nine, you may be told that it's simply because everyone does it. So it's a standard, model, or pattern regarded as typical that affects people's behavior at the workplace. When change or innovation efforts end certain norms, people firmly resist. Resistance will be particularly great when many people feel that the change upends their established sets of practice.

Yet there are two kinds of organizational norms: productive and unproductive. Here's a productive norm: everyone at our workplace is supposed to make clear to everyone else before going home what the plan is for the following day. Here's an unproductive norm: no one can go home until the boss gets ready to leave the office. We often stay until eleven at night, doing not very much.

People don't resist change when they're included in a discussion and come to a consensus about how to change an unproductive norm into one that's productive. When people's patterns are ignored or changed without their consent, they do resist. So the point here is to be sensitive and attentive to steps taken to change norms.

9. Lack of trust in the change initiator

People also resist change when the request for change comes from a person or persons they don't trust. They start questioning why this person has been put in charge of the project. When this is the situation, the project often fails.

10. Change that's too rapid

When excessive pressure is involved, people resist change. When ordered to make sweeping changes, they rebel even if they know change is needed. When people are pressured to produce results in an unreasonable amount of time, they tend to resist even more.

In this chapter, we shared our experiences according to Lippitt's views. These ten items could be used as a checklist when planning ways to prevent resistance to your idea implementation. In the next chapter, you'll find useful information that you'll be able to refer when promoting innovation efforts as a team leader.

CHAPTER 14

CHARACTERISTICS OF INNOVATIVE TEAM LEADERS

We once conducted a study of our client organizations to identify some common traits of people who were regarded among their peers as very innovative small-group leaders. We asked senior class managers, mainly in the area of R&D, about traits of project team leaders whom they regarded as innovative. The following is a summary of what we heard.

1. Encourage the group to become sensitive and responsive to changes

These leaders actively encourage junior team members to pay careful attention to changes in the environment that are related to their work. They make it a habit to raise the awareness of group members by frequently and spontaneously asking them questions like "Have you noticed anything new on the technology front lately?" "Do you know that our competitor just released a research paper?" "By the way, did you see this article, which appeared in a US journal recently?" To be sure, these leaders themselves are always on the alert regarding change and new developments.

2. Be thrilled and support new ideas

Innovative leaders are always ready to listen to the ideas of junior members. They try to point out positive aspects, however minor, and express enthusiasm when members present excellent ideas. In many cases, they express their support explicitly by saying, "I will support that, so just go ahead and give it a try."

3. Urge group members to avoid adhering to established practices

Leaders never stifle fresh ideas by advising group members to adhere to established practices. On the contrary, they show an ongoing interest in new approaches, examine how they might differ from existing practices, and adopt those that offer even a small measure of improvement. Their dedication to improvement is firm and forward looking, and when necessary, they warn group members of the dangers of stubbornly adhering to established patterns.

4. Encourage group members to take initiatives in learning

Innovative leaders motivate and fuel the group with incentives to learn. They frequently reach out to the group by posing questions, such as "Wouldn't you like to know about this? It's quite a promising field of the future. How about if we study it together?" Or these leaders are more specific in their suggestions, advising, "I would like you all to study this aspect by next month. This is going to be important for us in the near future." These leaders also hold frequent seminars and workshops. They themselves are eager to acquire knowledge and information, and they continually show this attitude to the group.

5. Purposefully encourage the innovation mentality

Leaders are mindful of maintaining an atmosphere in which the group feels the need to propose new ideas. Leaders encourage members to be forthcoming with ideas by challenging them with questions and comments like "Can you come up with a few new approaches for this?" or "Why don't you try a brand-new avenue on this one?"

6. Encourage knowledge acquisition in new subject fields

Leaders are always inquisitive and investigative about information for a subject topic they need to develop. They're particularly interested in newly emerging fields. They're likely to ask junior members to research and follow developments in new fields and make all-out efforts to see whether they can find new applications. They're also avid information gatherers, acquiring information not only in print and online but also through networking; attendance at seminars, conferences, and workshops; and in new subject areas, where possible. At their own firms, they're diligent, dedicated information gatherers through internal networking.

7. Listen intently to team members and be receptive to new ideas

No matter how busy they are, leaders make time to listen thoroughly to a team member who has a new idea. And they're always willing to support a new idea they consider worthwhile. They always make sure that the group is aware of their willingness to listen and openness to ideas.

8. Value all group opinions and appraise each well

When the group is discussing ideas, the leader has them hash it out from all angles and at times deliberately causes a full-scale argument, but he or she is in no hurry to have the group draw a conclusion. After collecting more information on the issue, the leader has the group discuss it further.

9. Keep the group mindful of value of innovation efforts

Leaders make efforts to point out cases of change and innovation taking place elsewhere, provide opportunities to discuss what needs to be done for their own innovation efforts, and asks for the group's opinions along with specific actions to take. They make members aware of what the organization could achieve by introducing new products and services, and applying new steps and procedures. They also actively search for new means, techniques, methodologies, and approaches that facilitate change and innovation.

10. Encourage group opinions to be constructive

Leaders value group opinions regarding, for example, how to overcome the shortage in personnel, time, budget, and technological capability. Rather than discouraging any idea, they demonstrate a highly positive attitude of wanting to work with the group to find solutions.

In this chapter, we summarized ten features of creative team leaders we found in Japan. Leaders with all the characteristics described above are rare. Yet these are the characteristics that describe leaders of innovation in most organizations.

PART IV

ACHIEVING SUSTAINED INNOVATION

CHAPTER 15

REQUIREMENTS FOR DEVELOPING AND DEMONSTRATING ORGANIZATIONAL CREATIVITY

In our final chapter, we would like share some of the things we've learned over years of research and consulting about what we believe is needed for developing and demonstrating organizational creativity. We believe that an organization must fulfill the following requirements to establish a solid foundation for maximizing the use of its human resources, specialist knowledge, and information.

1. Management orientation

1-1. Management and executives ensure that all employees are thoroughly familiar with the vision and aspirations of the organization. They also encourage the employees to propose new ideas toward that end and promise to examine their ideas.

1-2. Managers and executives have experience in new undertakings and make efforts from time to time to be clear to the employees on the importance of attempting something new.

1-3. The organization values highly those employees willing to take on a new challenge. The organization has a model that rejects the negatives such as "that's impossible" or "that's not possible at our company."

1-4. Organizational norms encourage individually structured, unofficial activities in addition to organized, official projects. In such cases, some resources (personnel, material, budget, time, and facilities) are made available without the need for the consent of a particular person or group.

2. Systems and rules

2-1. The company has a system that makes it easy for any employee to submit a new proposal.

2-2. Ideas from employees are promptly studied by a few staff and are returned to the proposer with comments and a decision on the viability of the idea. (Some organizations set up dedicated units called creative centers or innovation centers to receive, administer, and coordinate new proposals.)

2-3. To make idea proposals open to the organization at large, events such as idea rollouts, exhibitions, or technology shows are held to solicit idea-sponsoring departments or units.

If there's a creative center or innovation center, it's in charge of organizing such events.

2-4. Company-wide systems recognize excellent ideas. Two examples are a presidential award decided by the board of directors and a special award given by a top executive group—such as a commendation—and reported in a company bulletin or newsletter. (Some organizations give an award called Learned Contribution to recognize an idea that failed but contributed to the learning of the employees.)

2-5. Utilizing information technology, a system is established for the exchange of information. Ideas from both inside and outside the organization are stored there, and it's accessible for every employee to use for their own idea generation. (This system's design and architecture is becoming popular as a means of knowledge management.)

2-6. Networking arrangements are built into the company's structure for the exchange of ideas with other departments or organizations as well as networking gatherings or events to share or discuss technology.

3. Employees' and managers' orientation and intent

3-1. Most employees understand that new ideas and proposals are required not only from those in R&D and the planning department but also from those at every level in the entire organization.

3-2. A new initiative at the workplace is acknowledged without resistance. The employees are appreciative, interested, and cooperative.

3-3. Most employees understand the concept behind change and innovation efforts.

3-4. Most managers and employees actively participate in workshops to learn various methodologies and techniques.

3-5. The managers encourage and support activities of junior members in helping them produce new ideas.

3-6. Managers organize regular opportunities for junior members to discuss how to work better with people from other departments.

4. Encouragement, motivation, and communication

4-1. Seminars and training workshops make the employees aware of change and innovation.

4-2. The employees who are in indirect contact with the clients or trade partners are offered chances to make direct contact with the clients and partners along with their peer sales reps. This is meant to help enable employees with only indirect contact with clients to formulate ideas from the clients' standpoint.

4-3. Personnel rotation and staff reassignment occur often to give employees opportunities to get as much departmental work experience as possible. (Some organizations offer various work-experience opportunities, including interdepartmental networking events, in-house, interdepartmental training programs, innovation committees, and interdepartmental Innovation Meetings.)

Needless to say, few organizations fulfill all the pre-requisites listed above. Yet we can say, due to our long years of experience and research, that many innovative organizations exhibit many of the attributes on the list that are essential and vital to sustained innovation. With that said, we would like to say that we hope many of the measures, arrangements, and practices discussed here will help you in your future endeavors.

EPILOGUE

As mentioned in the preface, our concepts and methodologies for fostering innovative culture (individuals and organizations) were introduced around 1995 as a training program. We at Business Consultants, Inc., really appreciate and respect all authorities and experts who have inspired and taught us regarding innovation, creativity, and implementation that led us to develop this program.

In 2004, two books were published in Japanese based on this program. One is for concepts and the other is for techniques. In 2012, the essential parts of the book were organized into this book in English.

Now we're in a time of accelerating globalization with an increasing sense of anxiety regarding politics, economies, and society. In such an environment, no nation or organization can exist without innovation efforts.

Innovation is an easy word to use but is very difficult to put into practice. This has been proven true in many organizations and companies.

The methodologies we introduced in this book—idea inventing, screening, polishing, and mapping tools—

are applicable for individuals. You'll find that they're most effective if you work with other members in workshops. We provide open workshops and also trainer certification workshops.

Our mission in publishing this book and providing such workshops is to contribute to making the world, society, and organizations sustainable for future generations through supporting innovation efforts.

Thank you for reading this book. Please let us know you thoughts. And if you have any questions, please contact us.

E-mail: global@bcon.jp
Postal mail:
    Global Relations and Licensing Business
    Business Consultants, Inc.
    1-7-12 Sapia Tower 18th Fl., Marunouchi
    Chiyoda-ku, Tokyo 100-0005 Japan

BCon **Business Consultants, Inc.**

REFERENCES

Argyris, Chris. 1986. "Skilled Incompetence," *Harvard Business Review,* September-October.

Beckhard, R. 1997. *Agent of Change: My Life, My Practice.* San Francisco: Jossey-Bass.

Boylan, B. 2008. *What's Your Point?* Carbondale, Colo.: Point Publications.

Burke, W. W. 1982. *Organization Development: Principles and Practices.* Boston: Little, Brown and Company.

Drucker, P. F. 1993. *Management: Tasks, Responsibilities, Practices.* New York: HarperBusiness.

———. 2002. *Managing in the Next Society.* New York: St. Martin's Press.

Hersey, P., K. H. Blanchard, and D. E. Johnson. 2008. *Management of Organizational Behavior: Leading Human Resources.* 9th ed. Upper Saddle River, N.J.: Pearson Prentice Hall.

Lippitt, Gordon. 1975. Notes from a lecture of a presentation seminar titled "A Seminar Program with Dr. Gordon L. Lippitt and Dr. Cyril R. Mill," hosted by Business Consultants, Inc., Osaka and Tokyo, April 22-24, 28-30. Note: Lippitt later organized his research in his 1983 book, *A Handbook for Visual Problem Solving: A Resource Guide for Creating Change Models.* Bethesda, Md.: Development Publications.

Mintzberg, Henry. 1987. "Crafting Strategy," *Harvard Business Review,* July-August.

Mizutani, Masakazu. 1998. *Keieirinrigaku no susume.* Tokyo: Maruzen Library.

Nadlar, D. A., and M. L. Tushman. 1987. Presentation of this concept in an "OD program seminar" hosted by Business Consultants, Inc., in Tokyo and Osaka, April.

Nadler, D. A., R. B. Shaw, and A. E Walton. 1994. *Discontinuous Change.* San Francisco: Jossey-Bass.

Oech, R. V. 1998. *A Whack on the Side of the Head: How You Can Be More Creative.* 3rd ed. New York: Business Plus.

Osborn, A. F. 1963. *Applied Imagination: Principles and Procedures of Creative Problem-Solving.* 3rd rev. ed. New York: Charles Scribner's Sons.

Porter, M. E. 1980. *Competitive Strategy.* New York: Free Press.

Rhinesmith, S. H. 1996. *A Manager's Guide to Globalization.* Illinois: IRWIN Professional Publishing.

Roberts, E. B., and A. R. Fusfeld, 1982. "Critical Functions: Needed Roles in the Innovation Process." In *Career issues in human resource management.* Edited by R. Katz, pp. 186-187. New Jersey: Prentice-Hall.

Senge, P. M. 1990. *The Fifth Discipline: The Art and Practice of the Learning Organization.* New York: Currency.

Shannon, C. E. 1948. "A Mathematical Theory of Communication." *The Bell System Technical Journal* 27, July–October.

Shibao, Yoshiaki. 1999. *Project Management Kakushin: Jinzai—Process—Tool no Saiteki Katsuyo.* Tokyo: Seisansei Shuppan.

Tushman, M. L., and C. A. O'Reilly. 1997. *Winning Through Innovation: A Practical Guide to Leading Organizational Change and Renewal.* Boston: Harvard Business School Press.

www.ingramcontent.com/pod-product-compliance
Lightning Source LLC
Chambersburg PA
CBHW051504170526
45166CB00001B/379